Application

THE VAULT DWELLER'S
OFFICIAL
COOKBOOK

THE VAULT DWELLER'S
OFFICIAL
COOKBOOK

by Victoria Rosenthal

INSIGHT
EDITIONS

San Rafael, California

CONTENTS

INTRODUCTION

Welcome to Vault-Tec™ Life!

Let Vault-Tec be the first to welcome you to your new home, your new family, and your new life! We understand that it can be a challenge transitioning away from a world that, if you are reading this, has surely come to an end. However, you've made the right choice in selecting Vault-Tec's premium survival shelters as your new home. We are doing all that we can to make you and your family comfortable and safe. Vault-Tec takes pride in our fine vault communities, but your new home here at Vault *[NUMBER NOT FOUND]* is guaranteed to be our very best. We hope you enjoy your stay with us and remember to always follow the orders of your local Overseer. An orderly vault is a happy vault.

We hope all of the mandatory reading you have been assigned has been educational and enlightening. In this document, we will discuss everyone's favorite place in the home: the kitchen! All of our Vault-Tec kitchens are equipped with every modern luxury you could hope for. Why, you won't even remember your old, dated, irradiated kitchen when you see what Vault-Tec has in store for you. We've made sure to include a state-of-the-art Mister Handy in every kitchen, ready to assist you in any way. The information inside this instructional manual has already been programmed into the unit, so don't hesitate to ask him questions, day or night.

As you settle in for your short stay with us, we want to share a few of our own specially designed Vault-Tec-approved recipes. We have included all of your classic favorites along with dazzling dishes of tomorrow. A hearty meal is essential to keeping you happy and healthy, and this vault needs strong, able bodies to function. Take pride in your meals as they are the fuel of our future!

ENTERTAINING, THE VAULT-TEC™ WAY

Just because your life has been reduced to seeing the same faces for the foreseeable future doesn't mean you should neglect one of the most important duties of a homeowner: being a gracious host! We want to make sure that all of the most fulfilling aspects of a civil society carry on. Being in such a confined space, it's important to treat each of your fellow vault dwellers with courtesy and respect, so please review these notes on proper vault etiquette.

BASIC FAMILY MEAL

Meal time with the family is one of the most important parts of your day. Sitting at the dining table with a warm roast and a cool drink is one of the best ways for your family to connect, ensuring a lifetime of happiness. Maybe young Billy will want to talk about the new friends he made in the classroom today. Or does Jane want you to know about the new crush she has? Oh ho, you haven't heard about that one yet? Do make sure your children are acting appropriately and please report any suspicious activities to the vault Overseer. While you are at it, pass around another helping of the InstaMash!

SMALL PARTY IN THE VAULT

Is it your vault-mate's birthday? Did the scientists in your vault just complete another successful experiment? What better way to celebrate small victories than to hold a small party with your new best friends. Prepare one of our delicious Vault-Tec entrees and make enough to share with everyone! Please note that a small party can consist of no more than eight (8) dwellers or you will need to fill out the proper paperwork to register a large gathering. Your assigned Mister Handy may even know a few parlor tricks with which to entertain your guests!

LARGE GATHERING

For larger gatherings in the vault, it is best to share responsibilities. After the paperwork is filled out and the room is reserved, you are ready to celebrate with your fellow vault dwellers. One of our favorite methods of hosting a large group is with a delicious potluck. Post a sign-up sheet and let partygoers volunteer to cook and bring different dishes. Variety is the spice of life, so bring those unique dishes to the party for all to try. Do make sure to properly schedule your time in the kitchen, as cooking is a privilege that can be revoked at any time.

DIETARY RESTRICTIONS

Each vault has been stocked to the brim with food and supplies to make your stay an enjoyable one. We understand some of our dwellers have dietary restrictions and we have made sure to provide a variety of substitutions. Although our Vault-Tec scientists have made some progress on meat-substitute paste, we do not consider ourselves experts on these restrictions and hope you use these recipes as a starting point and adjust to your liking.

ADAPTING TO VEGETARIAN DIETS

Several recipes in this book start off vegetarian friendly. Many others can be adapted to your dietary needs. Feel free to replace meat broth with vegetable broth. Swap out the protein with your favorite grilled vegetable or meat substitute (this will affect the cooking times) and dig in.

ADAPTING TO GLUTEN-FREE DIETS

An allergy to gluten can make navigating the food pantry dangerous. Lucky for you, we have kept your needs a priority and have stocked each vault with a plethora of alternatives. These include coconut flour, cornstarch, potato flour, quinoa, and many others. For most recipes you will be able to use equal ratios of gluten-free substitute to flour, but be prepared to modify the quantity just in case. Make sure to share your successes with the head chef of the vault.

ADAPTING TO LACTOSE-FREE DIETS

Those unable to digest the natural sugars found in dairy products should not fear recipes filled with butter and milk. Replace milk and heavy cream with coconut, almond, soy, or any of your favorite non-dairy options. Replace butter with equal portions of the supplied non-dairy margarine options found in our storerooms. We stocked too much margarine—please take some! We could always use more space for oxygen tanks.

To receive access to any of these products, speak with your Overseer or vault staff. Remember to be creative and share your delicious findings with your fellow vault dwellers. Do not limit yourself by strictly following these recipes. Experimentation is half the fun! The other half eludes our scientists.

COOKING AFTER THE VAULT

All good things must come to an end, and before you know it your time with us will be over. We'd love to have you stay in perpetuity, but once the global radioactive contamination has abated and you receive the All Clear Signal, you'll be able to leave the vault to begin your new life and start rebuilding our great nation. Don't worry, Vault-Tec would never dream of sending you on your way without offering some words of wisdom for the road ahead.

Although it is difficult to anticipate exactly how nuclear fallout will affect the outside world, our scientists have analyzed the possibilities and have come up with helpful hints and practices to aid you on your post-vault adventure. Regardless of the apocalyptic circumstance, these suggestions will get you on your feet and ready to journey into the new world.

GATHERING INGREDIENTS

Mother nature is one tough lady, and vegetation will certainly still exist in some form or another. As you set off into the great unknown, it will be important to take note of how the world has changed since you were last on the surface. It could be that nature has reclaimed the once-great cities of the world and the food will be plentiful! You may also emerge into a bleak wasteland, pitted with craters and ash, home to nothing but irradiated shrubs and an ocean of sand. Remember, adversity builds character!

The fruits and vegetables you have grown up with may not exist, or they may have mutated into more interesting varieties, so you'll need to work with what you can find. Feel free to annotate this book with any ingredients that serve as suitable substitutes in our recipes. Do be careful when experimenting with new vegetation, and make sure you have a few Stimpaks and Rad-X handy, as you'll want to stay strong and healthy.

Be sure to take caution when approaching any wildlife that you may encounter. If animals display aggressive behavior, assert your dominance. Your RobCo Pip-Boy is equipped with a Vault-Tec Assigned Targeting System (V.A.T.S.) to help you approach any dangers you come across. Use it to determine the optimal course of action, and fire away! Look at you, a regular hunter. After defeating your target, you will want to butcher the best cuts for some delicious cooking in the future. Be cautious if any meat has an unexpected odor or looks green in color. Remember, green means stop, red means go!

PREPARING AND COOKING

After you have gathered your ingredients, take a look through the pages of this manual for some delicious ideas. Campfires and camping stoves make for nifty oven replacements on the road. To set up a basic campfire, simply refer to page 226 in your *Vault-Tec Survival Guide* for more information. Once you get your fire going strong, you will need to place a grate above the flames to act as a stovetop. You are now on your way to cooking a quality Vault-Tec-inspired meal on the road.

BASICS

Before we get started, here are a few basic recipes you'll find helpful throughout this cookbook!

THIS IS A BIT OF AN ECLECTIC LIST, BUT HELPFUL NONETHELESS.

CHICKEN BROTH

1 whole chicken

Salt

Pepper

2 onions, quartered

3 celery ribs, cut into large pieces

6 garlic cloves

One 3-inch piece fresh ginger

2 lemongrass stalks

1 cinnamon stick

1 bunch parsley

3 quarts (12 cups) water, divided

2 tablespoons tomato paste

1 teaspoon sugar

RAD CHICKENS ARE EASY TO CATCH, BUT APPROACH THEM CAREFULLY BECAUSE THEY CAN BE FAST.

BLACK BLOODLEAF WOULD PROBABLY ADD A NICE ZING TO THIS RECIPE.

1. Preheat the oven to 400°F. Season the whole chicken with salt and pepper, inside and out. Place the chicken, onion, celery, garlic, ginger, lemongrass, and cinnamon stick in a 7.25-quart ovenproof pot and roast, uncovered, for 1 hour and 15 minutes. Remove the pot from the oven and let the chicken cool enough to handle. Remove the chicken breast and place in the refrigerator, covered, to make soup later.

2. Break down the chicken by removing the limbs and splitting the chest cavity. Place the chicken parts, parsley, and 2 quarts of the water into the pot used for roasting. In a small bowl, combine the tomato paste, sugar and about 2 tablespoons of the water. Add the tomato paste mixture to the pot and stir to combine.

3. Bring the broth to a boil over medium-high heat then reduce the heat to low. Keep at a slight simmer, uncovered, for 4 hours. Make sure to occasionally add water to keep the liquid level consistent. After the broth has simmered for 4 hours, carefully strain into another container to separate the broth from all the ingredients. Cover the broth and refrigerate overnight.

4. The next day, take the broth out of the refrigerator and the fat will have settled at the top. Remove this layer of fat and the broth is ready to use. You may also save some of the fat to add a little extra flavor to any soups you make.

Used in: Radgull Power Noodles (page 45), Chicken Noodle Soup (page 51)

NUKA-COLA BBQ SAUCE

Who would have guessed you could make such a delicious sauce with a few ingredients and Nuka-Cola?

½ cup Nuka-Cola soda (page 165)

½ cup ketchup

¼ cup Worcestershire sauce

¼ cup steak sauce

1 teaspoon onion powder

1 teaspoon garlic powder

1 tablespoon hot sauce

1. Combine all the ingredients in a large saucepan over medium-high heat. Bring to a boil and then reduce the heat to low. Simmer uncovered for 20 minutes. Transfer to an airtight container, cover, and store in the refrigerator for up to 1 month.

Used in: Baked Bloatfly (page 83), Dusty's Brahmin Burgers (page 89)

CARAMEL BUTTERCREAM FROSTING

1 cup (2 sticks) unsalted butter, at room temperature

½ cup caramel sauce

1 teaspoon salt

2 to 4 cups confectioners' sugar

1. In a bowl of a stand mixer fitted with the paddle attachment, whip the butter until smooth.

2. Add the salt and caramel and whisk until combined. Add the confectioners' sugar 1 cup at a time. Continue to add confectioners' sugar until you are happy with the flavor and the thickness of the frosting.

Used in: Perfectly Preserved Pie (page 127)

APPETIZERS

YUMYUM DEVILED EGGS

Ten out of ten Vault-Tec™ doctors agree, a YumYum Brand Pure Dried
Whole Deviled Egg a day keeps the atom bombs at bay.

*THE DOCTOR'S ROOM WAS FULL
OF IMPRESSIVE PIECES OF PAPER
SO IT MUST BE TRUE...*

S.P.E.C.I.A.L: +1
AGILITY FOR 1 HOUR

DIFFICULTY:
EASY

PREP TIME:
15 MINUTES

COOK TIME:
15 MINUTES

SERVINGS:
12 DEVILED EGGS

PAIRS WELL WITH:
MYSTERY MEAT–WRAPPED
NUKALURK (PAGE 31)

6 eggs

½ cup mayonnaise

1 tablespoon miso paste

¼ teaspoon ground coriander

½ teaspoon ground cumin

¼ teaspoon ground turmeric

½ teaspoon ground mustard

¼ teaspoon cayenne pepper

¼ teaspoon ground fennel

Salt and black pepper

Fresh minced chives for garnishing

1. Place the eggs in a large pot and fill with enough water to completely cover. Cover with
   a lid and place over medium-high heat. Bring the water to a boil and start a timer for 8
   minutes. Fill a large bowl with ice cubes and water.

2. Once the timer for the eggs has gone off, immediately take the pot off the stove and place
   it under cold running water. Move the contents to the bowl with the ice cubes. Carefully
   remove the shells from the eggs.

3. Cut the eggs in half. Place the egg yolks in a bowl with the mayonnaise and miso.
   Combine the ingredients until smooth. Add the coriander, cumin, turmeric, mustard,
   cayenne pepper, and fennel. Season to taste with salt and black pepper.

4. Spoon the egg yolk mixture into each of the egg white halves. Garnish with chives.

MIRELURK BELLY
~~SALMON~~ CROQUETTES

Salmon croquettes are a classic dish, the perfect appetizer to share with all!

I MANAGED TO GROW MY OWN LITTLE PATCH OF POTATOES FROM THE SPUD I "BORROWED" FROM THE RIVET CITY SCIENCE LAB, BUT I CAN'T MAKE THIS RECIPE TOO OFTEN. I DON'T THINK THEY'LL LET ME "BORROW" ANOTHER ONE.

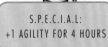

2 tablespoons unsalted butter

½ medium yellow onion, diced

¾ cup plus 2 tablespoons all-purpose flour, divided

¼ teaspoon ground allspice

1 teaspoon garlic powder

½ teaspoon ground cinnamon

1 teaspoon salt

¼ teaspoon pepper

½ cup milk

2 large russet potatoes, peeled, cooked, and mashed

1 pound smoked salmon, flaked

3 scallions, both green and white parts finely diced

3 eggs, lightly beaten

1 cup panko bread crumbs

Peanut oil, for frying

TWO WHOLE FRESH POTATOES FOR THIS RECIPE! THIS IS ONE OF THE MOST EXPENSIVE MEALS IN THIS BOOK.

> **S.P.E.C.I.A.L:**
> +1 AGILITY FOR 4 HOURS

> **DIFFICULTY:**
> MEDIUM
>
> **PREP TIME:**
> 30 MINUTES
>
> **COOK TIME:**
> 1 HOUR
>
> **SERVINGS:**
> 16 TO 24
>
> **PAIRS WELL WITH:**
> CREAMY GARLIC SAUCE

1. Heat a large sauté pan or skillet over medium-high heat and add the unsalted butter. Once the butter has melted, add the diced onions and cook until translucent, about 5 minutes. Add 2 tablespoons of the flour and the allspice, garlic powder, cinnamon, salt, and pepper and mix until well combined.

2. Slowly add the milk and stir until thickened. Remove from the heat and combine with the mashed potatoes. Mix in the smoked salmon and scallions.

3. Form into 16 to 24 equal-sized patties and place on a baking tray lined with parchment paper. The mixture will be a little wet. Refrigerate, uncovered, for 1 hour.

4. Prepare 3 bowls for breading the croquettes. Fill the first bowl with the remaining ¾ cup flour, fill the second with the lightly beaten eggs, and fill the third with the panko. Coat all sides of each patty in flour, then in egg, and finally in panko.

5. Pour 2 inches of peanut oil in a deep pot and heat to 375°F. Carefully place several of the croquettes at a time into the hot oil. Fry each side for 2 to 3 minutes, until golden brown.

MOLE RAT WONDER MEAT DIP

This delicious dip is the perfect addition to any vault party!

RYAN BRIGG IS EITHER A CULINARY GENIUS OR A MAD SCIENTIST. THERE'S NO WAY HE CAN MAKE SOMETHING SO DELICIOUS WITH ONLY MOLE RAT AND WONDERGLUE. I WISH I COULD GET MY HANDS ON THAT WONDER MEAT MAKER OF HIS, BUT HIS BAND OF RAIDERS POSES A PROBLEM. THIS RECIPE WILL HAVE TO DO UNTIL I FIGURE OUT HIS SECRET.

S.P.E.C.I.A.L:
+1 CHARISMA
FOR 30 MINUTES

DIFFICULTY:
EASY

PREP TIME:
30 MINUTES

COOK TIME:
30 MINUTES

SERVINGS:
5

PAIRS WELL WITH:
CRUSTY BREAD

¼ cup (½ stick) unsalted butter

5 garlic cloves, minced

4 scallions, white and light green parts, chopped

2 Italian sausages, casings removed and roughly chopped

MOLE RAT MEAT SEEMS TO HAVE THE SAME CONSISTENCY AS THIS "ITALIAN SAUSAGE." LUMPY AND PINK!

Two 8.5-ounce cans artichoke hearts, roughly chopped

2 cups cream cheese, at room temperature

CREAM CHEESE? THIS MUST BE SOME SORT OF PRE-WAR ADHESIVE. REPLACE WITH ½ CUP WONDERGLUE.

½ cup grated Parmesan cheese

1 cup shredded fontina cheese

Salt and pepper

1. Preheat the oven to 375°F. Melt the butter in a large sauté pan or skillet over medium-high heat. Add the garlic and scallions and cook for 5 minutes, until fragrant. Mix in the chopped Italian sausage and cook until no longer pink. Add the artichoke hearts and cook for another 5 minutes, until soft. Drain any liquid and set aside.

2. Combine the cream cheese, Parmesan cheese, and fontina cheese in a medium bowl until smooth. Add the sausage mixture and mix well. Season to taste with salt and pepper. Place in a 1-quart baking dish and bake for 20 minutes. Turn the broiler on and broil until the top browns, about 2 to 3 minutes.

SHRIMP-STUFFED MUSHROOMS

I'VE NEVER SEEN A REAL SHRIMP, BUT BASED ON REFERENCE PICTURES, I FIGURE A HERMIT CRAB FROM FAR HARBOR WOULD WORK JUST AS WELL. THEY LOOK SORT OF SIMILAR, AND EVEN BETTER, YOU WON'T HAVE TO SHELL AND DEVEIN A BUNCH OF INDIVIDUAL SHRIMP. YOU JUST HAVE TO KILL ONE CRAB AND PRY IT OUT OF ITS LOBSTER GRILL FAMILY RESTAURANT TRUCK SHELL.

S.P.E.C.I.A.L:
+1 CHARISMA
FOR 30 MINUTES

20 large baby portobello mushrooms, stemmed

3.5 ounces cooked shrimp, minced

½ cup bread crumbs

½ cup cream cheese

2 chopped scallions

2 teaspoons garlic powder

¼ cup grated Parmesan cheese

¼ cup grated Romano cheese

1 teaspoon dried oregano

½ teaspoon salt

¼ teaspoon pepper

IF YOU USE GLOWING FUNGUS CAPS, THIS DISH ADDS A BEAUTIFUL AMBIANCE TO THE MEAL.

DIFFICULTY:
EASY

PREP TIME:
15 MINUTES

COOK TIME:
20 MINUTES

SERVINGS:
12

PAIRS WELL WITH:
RANCH DRESSING

1. Preheat the oven to 350°F. Spread the mushrooms on a baking sheet and bake for 15 minutes, until the mushrooms release a bit of liquid. Remove from the oven and remove any liquid on the baking sheet.

2. Combine the remaining ingredients in a medium bowl. Fill each mushroom cap with a tablespoon of the mixture.

3. Bake uncovered for 30 to 35 minutes, until the filling is browned. These are best served warm.

ROLLED ~~HAM~~ OMELET

IT'S HARD TO FIND CHICKEN EGGS JUST LYING AROUND, BUT DEATHCLAW NESTS ARE EVERYWHERE! SUBSTITUTE SIX PRE-WAR EGGS WITH TWO DEATHCLAW EGGS IN THIS RECIPE.

S.P.E.C.I.A.L:
+1 INTELLIGENCE
FOR 1 HOUR

DIFFICULTY:
MEDIUM

PREP TIME:
1 HOUR

COOK TIME:
30 MINUTES

SERVINGS:
12 PIECES

PAIRS WELL WITH:
HOLLANDAISE SAUCE

OMELET

½ cup heavy cream

¼ cup cream cheese, at room temperature

6 eggs

2 tablespoons chives, minced

3 tablespoons all-purpose flour

½ teaspoon onion powder

¼ teaspoon paprika

½ cup finely chopped ham

PIGS ARE ALSO HARD TO COME BY. IT'S BEST TO REPLACE HAM MEAT WITH DEATHCLAW THIGHS. SO MEATY.

SLAW

¼ cup mayonnaise

¼ cup Greek yogurt

2 tablespoons honey

3 tablespoons rice vinegar

1 teaspoon celery salt

1 cup shredded apple

2 cups (about 3 whole)
  peeled and julienned carrots

TO MAKE THE OMELET:

1. Preheat the oven to 375°F and line a 15-by-10-inch baking pan with parchment paper and nonstick cooking spray. Whisk together the cream cheese and heavy cream in a bowl. Add the eggs and whisk until fluffy. Add the chives, flour, onion powder, paprika, and ham, and mix to combine.

2. Pour the egg mixture into the prepared pan. Bake for 15 to 18 minutes, until egg is set. Allow to cool.

TO MAKE THE SLAW:

3. Combine the mayonnaise, yogurt, honey, rice vinegar, and celery salt in a medium bowl. Add the apple and carrot and toss to combine. Refrigerate until you are ready to serve.

TO ASSEMBLE:

4. Take the cooled omelet and top evenly with the slaw.

5. Gently loosen the edges of the omelet from the pan. Then, beginning from the short edge of the pan, carefully roll the omelet up, separating the egg from the parchment paper as you do so. Tightly wrap the omelet roll in plastic wrap and refrigerate for at least 1 hour.

6. Take the roll out of the refrigerator and remove the plastic wrap, then slice it into 2-inch pieces. Carefully dry any juice that may have escaped from the slaw with a paper towel.

MEAT KEBABS

After thousands of hours and millions of dollars spent, Vault-Tec™ is proud to bring you the ultimate recipe for kebabs, better known as meat-on-a-stick. Duck produced the best results, but any meat will do, really.

S.P.E.C.I.A.L:
+1 ENDURANCE
FOR 30 MINUTES

DIFFICULTY:
MEDIUM

PREP TIME:
1 HOUR

COOK TIME:
30 MINUTES

SERVING SIZE:
3

PAIRS WELL WITH:
TZATZIKI SAUCE,
PITA BREAD

5 garlic cloves

½ cup olive oil

2 tablespoons red wine vinegar

1 tablespoon honey

2 teaspoons dried oregano

½ teaspoon ground ginger

2 (7.5-ounce) duck breasts,
    cut into large bite-size pieces

½ red onion, quartered and layers separated

THIS IS AMAZING WITH ANY MEAT. IT EVEN MAKES STRINGY IGUANA BITS EDIBLE.

1. Place the garlic cloves, olive oil, red wine vinegar, honey, oregano, and ginger in a food processor and blend until well combined to create a marinade.

2. Place the duck breasts in a zip-top bag, pour the marinade in, and refrigerate for at least 2 hours, turning the bag over every hour.

3. Thirty minutes prior to grilling, soak wooden skewers in water.

4. Remove the duck meat from the marinade. Place a piece of meat on a skewer followed by 2 pieces of red onion. Repeat until you have 7 pieces of meat on the stick.

5. Preheat a grill to high.

6. Cook the skewers for 5 to 10 minutes, flipping occasionally, until all sides are crisp.

MYSTERY MEAT-WRAPPED NUKALURK
BACON-WRAPPED SCALLOPS

Scientists have found that wrapping something with bacon increases the deliciousness factor and savory quotient by over 48 percent, resulting in this delectable recipe.

PICKED UP SOME MYSTERY BACON FROM THE RAIDERS AT NUKA-WORLD. AT LEAST, THEY TOLD ME IT WAS BACON. I DON'T THINK I SAW A SINGLE PIG WHEN I WAS THERE. I GUESS THAT MUST BE THE MYSTERY.

12 sea scallops

3 tablespoons unsalted butter, melted

⅓ cup brown sugar

1 teaspoon ground cumin

1 teaspoon ground fenugreek

¼ teaspoon cayenne pepper

6 thin bacon slices, halved   MYSTERY BACON

Salt and black pepper

THE NUKALURK'S BELLY PAIRS EXTREMELY WELL WITH THE MYSTERY BACON THE RAIDERS OF NUKA-WORLD SHARED WITH ME. IT ALSO GIVES THIS DISH A NICE BLUE GLOW.

S.P.E.C.I.A.L:
+1 ENDURANCE FOR 1 HOUR

DIFFICULTY:
EASY

PREP TIME:
10 MINUTES

COOK TIME:
10 MINUTES

SERVINGS:
12

PAIRS WELL WITH:
SPICY MAYONNAISE

1. Preheat the oven to 425°F. In a large bowl, toss the scallops in the melted butter.

2. In a separate large bowl, combine the brown sugar, cumin, fenugreek, and cayenne pepper. Place the bacon slices in the bowl and toss to season generously.

3. Wrap a slice of bacon around each scallop and pierce with a toothpick to secure. Sprinkle salt and pepper over the wrapped scallops.

4. Place all the scallops on a rack in a deep baking dish. Roast in the oven for 15 minutes. Flip and roast for another 15 minutes, until scallops are cooked through and bacon is crispy.

SCOTCH EGGS ~BRAHMIN FRIES~

In the event of nuclear war, we at Vault-Tec™ want to make sure
we preserve a record of some of the cultural treats found elsewhere.
This recipe is the best of British cuisine.

My journeys out West brought me to a charming establishment called
Mom's Diner. One particularly unenthused patron suggested I stay
away from the Brahmin fries, but I couldn't help myself and ordered
a plate. These are . . . not the same recipe, but I much prefer this to
harvesting the Brahmin, uh, "meat" myself from one of the beasts.

S.P.E.C.I.A.L:
+2 STRENGTH
FOR 3 HOURS

DIFFICULTY:
HARD

PREP TIME:
1 HOUR

COOK TIME:
20 MINUTES

SERVINGS:
8

PAIRS WELL WITH:
SWEET MUSTARD SAUCE

1 pound ground beef

¾ pound ground lamb

1 tablespoon ground mustard

2 teaspoons garlic powder

2 teaspoons dried thyme

1 tablespoon onion powder

¼ teaspoon ground nutmeg

1 teaspoon salt

1 teaspoon pepper

⅔ cup all-purpose flour

2 eggs, beaten

1 cup panko bread crumbs

8 soft-boiled or hard-boiled eggs

Peanut oil for frying

1. Combine the ground beef, ground lamb, ground mustard, garlic powder, thyme, onion powder, nutmeg, salt, and pepper in a large bowl. Mix with your hands to combine and separate into eight equal portions.

2. Place three wide, shallow bowls on your work surface. Add the flour to the first bowl, beaten eggs to the second, and panko crumbs to the third.

3. Take a boiled egg and roll it in the flour to coat. Take a portion of the ground meat and flatten it. Place the egg in the center and carefully wrap the meat around the egg so it is completely covered. Repeat this with the remaining eggs.

4. Dip each meat-wrapped egg in the beaten eggs, and finally in the panko. Be sure to cover the meat completely with crumbs.

5. Pour 2 inches of peanut oil into a deep pot and preheat the oil to 350°F.

6. Once the oil has reached the correct temperature, carefully place 2 of the balls into the oil. Allow them to fry for 5 minutes, turning regularly until all sides are golden brown. Remove and place on a plate covered with a paper towel to drain any excess oil. Repeat with the remaining eggs.

MIRELURK CLAW
~~CRAB~~ CAKES

The meatiest part of a crab is the claw, but cracking them open is such a hassle!
In your spacious new vault you'll find that we've provided easy-to-open cans of
lump crabmeat that will make this recipe a breeze.

*I LOOKED UP CRABS IN THE ARCHIVES AND FOUND AN ENTRY FOR
SMALL AQUATIC CREATURES WITH PINCERS. I CAN'T GET NEAR THE
WATER WITH ALL OF THE MIRELURKS IN THE WAY. THEY'VE GOT
PINCERS AS WELL AND LOOK PRETTY MEATY TO ME. I THINK A RIFLE
BUTT WOULD WORK JUST FINE AS A CLAW CRACKER, TOO.*

S.P.E.C.I.A.L:
+2 AGILITY FOR 3 HOURS

DIFFICULTY:
MEDIUM

PREP TIME:
30 MINUTES

COOK TIME:
20 MINUTES

SERVINGS:
8

PAIRS WELL WITH:
SPICY MAYONNAISE

⅓ cup mayonnaise

¼ cup Dijon mustard

1 teaspoon Worcestershire sauce

2 teaspoons lemon juice

Zest of 1 lemon

1 teaspoon celery salt

¼ teaspoon pepper

¼ teaspoon ground ginger

Pinch of ground nutmeg

¼ teaspoon red pepper flakes

Pinch of ground allspice

15.5 ounces ~~crabmeat~~ *MIRELURK CLAW MEAT*

1 egg

2 scallions, chopped

1 cup panko bread crumbs

1 tablespoon canola oil

1. Combine the mayonnaise, Dijon mustard, Worcestershire sauce, lemon zest, lemon juice, celery salt, pepper, ginger, nutmeg, red pepper flakes, and allspice in a large bowl. Add the crabmeat, egg, scallions, and panko and mix together so all ingredients are well combined. Form the meat into 8 equal-sized 1-inch-thick crab cakes.

2. Heat the oil in a large sauté pan or skillet over medium-high. Place the crab cakes in the pan and cook until golden brown on both sides, about 3 to 5 minutes per side.

DESERT SALAD

This classic salad recipe is a Vault-Tec™ favorite and will cover all of your essential food pyramid needs, from your daily recommended dose of green vegetables to your daily mandatory intake of cumin. Increase or reduce ingredient portions to taste.

WHAT IS A FOOD PYRAMID? REMIND ME TO CHECK THE INVENTORY MANIFEST FOR A PYRAMID LATER.

1 medium yellow onion, chopped

1 pound ~~extra-lean ground beef~~ *GROUND BRAHMIN*

3 tablespoons ground cumin

1 tablespoon chili powder

½ teaspoon smoked paprika

3 teaspoons garlic powder

Salt and black pepper

1 head iceberg lettuce, roughly chopped

1 cup cooked pinto beans, drained and rinsed

1 cup corn kernels

10 small tomatoes, cut into bite-size slices

One 3-ounce can sliced black olives

½ cup shredded cheddar cheese

1 medium shallot, thinly sliced

2 avocados (optional)

One 8-ounce bottle prepared Catalina dressing

Queso fresco for serving

Tortilla chips for serving

S.P.E.C.I.A.L:
+2 INTELLIGENCE
FOR 3 HOURS

DIFFICULTY:
MEDIUM

PREP TIME:
1 HOUR

COOK TIME:
15 MINUTES

SERVINGS:
4

PAIRS WELL WITH:
BLUE CORNBREAD
MUFFINS (PAGE 69)

1. In a large sauté pan or skillet pan, cook the onion and ground beef over medium heat until the meat is no longer pink. Drain the fat from the pan, then season with the cumin, chili powder, smoked paprika, and garlic powder. Season with salt and pepper to taste.

2. In a large bowl, toss together the iceberg lettuce, pinto beans, corn, tomatoes, olives, cheddar cheese, and shallot. This can be refrigerated until ready to serve.

3. To serve, dice the avocados and toss with the salad. Add a small portion of the dressing and toss with the salad. Portion out the salad on individual plates and top with the warm beef, a drizzle of queso fresco, and crushed tortilla chips.

SOUPS AND STEWS

Bobrov Brothers' **CABBAGE SOUP**

The vault is filled with all of your favorite prepackaged favorites, but if you have a hankering for some vegetables for some reason, this nutritious cabbage soup is a great choice.

During my travels, I stopped by the Dugout Inn, where I cooked up this recipe in exchange for a place to sleep. Vadim Bobrov kept saying that it reminded him of his younger days with his grandmother. He kept talking as he slurped up a bowl, and he mentioned he's adding it to the menu.

¼ cup (½ stick) unsalted butter

1 medium onion, diced

1 medium shallot, diced

1 celery rib, diced

1 medium carrot, peeled and grated

½ head green cabbage, sliced thin

½ head purple cabbage, sliced thin

2 quarts (8 cups) vegetable broth

1 bay leaf

4 red potatoes, peeled and cubed

2 plum tomatoes, seeded and chopped

1 tablespoon fresh parsley, measured then chopped

Salt and pepper

I've seen some huge mutated cabbages being grown over on the West Coast in New California.

"Plum tomato"? Is that what happens when a tato and a pear mutate together?

S.P.E.C.I.A.L:
+1 CHARISMA
FOR 1 HOUR

DIFFICULTY:
MEDIUM

PREP TIME:
45 MINUTES

COOK TIME:
45 MINUTES

SERVINGS:
8

PAIRS WELL WITH:
BUTTERED RYE BREAD

1. Melt the butter in a large pot over medium-high heat. Add the onion, shallot, and celery, then cook until softened, about 5 minutes. Add the carrot and cabbage. Stir and cook for 5 minutes. Add the vegetable broth and bay leaf, then bring to a boil. Reduce the heat to low, cover, and simmer for 20 minutes.

2. Add the potatoes and simmer for another 15 minutes until the potatoes are tender. Increase the heat, add the tomatoes, and bring to a boil. Reduce the heat again, cover, and simmer for 10 minutes. Remove the bay leaf. Add the parsley and season to taste with salt and pepper.

GULPER SLURRY

CLAM CHOWDER

Thanks to the tenacious persistence of a Vault-Tec™ Regional HQ in Boston, we are including a clam chowder recipe for all vault dwellers to enjoy. Select vaults will now be supplied with no fewer than 10,000 cans of clams in order to meet the demands of Boston HQ.*

3 slices thick-cut bacon

1 medium yellow onion, chopped

3 garlic cloves, minced

2 celery ribs, chopped

Two 10-ounce cans whole clams

1 cup vegetable broth

2 bay leaves

1 teaspoon dried thyme

3 yukon gold potatoes, peeled and cubed

1 cup heavy cream

1 cup half-and-half

2 teaspoons Worcestershire sauce

2 tablespoons cornstarch

2 tablespoons water

Salt and pepper

S.P.E.C.I.A.L:
+1 INTELLIGENCE
FOR 1 HOUR

DIFFICULTY:
MEDIUM

PREP TIME:
30 MINUTES

COOK TIME:
45 MINUTES

SERVINGS:
4

PAIRS WELL WITH:
CRACKERS, BREAD BOWL

1. Heat a dutch oven over medium heat and lay the bacon strips flat across the bottom. Cook the bacon until crispy. Remove the strips and let them drain on a plate lined with paper towels. Crumble and set aside.

2. Add the onion, garlic, and celery to the dutch oven and cook in the rendered bacon fat over medium until softened, about 5 minutes. Drain the juice from the cans of clam into the dutch oven, and set the clam meat aside. Add the vegetable broth, bay leaves, thyme, and potatoes and turn heat up to medium-high to bring to a simmer. Cover and reduce heat to medium-low and cook for 15 minutes, until the potatoes are tender.

3. Stir in the clams, heavy cream, half-and-half, and Worcestershire sauce. Remove the bay leaves. Season with salt and pepper. Heat on medium until the soup is warm, but do not boil. In a small bowl, stir the cornstarch and the water together to make a slurry. Add the slurry to the soup and stir until the soup has thickened. Top each serving with the crumbled bacon.

*Note: In order to make the necessary space for the clams in Vault Warehouses, the amount of medical and operational resources for each vault has been reduced accordingly. WELL, SHIT.

DUCK CURRY UDON

Enjoy this warm and comforting noodle soup if your climate-controlled vault ever dips below its perfectly programmed balmy 72 degrees.

Takahashi is a master of the noodle dish and this soup is close to the pricy bowl of noodles I ordered from him once. It's just too bad I can't ask him what the secret to his soup is in Japanese.

ROUX:

¼ cup all-purpose flour

1½ tablespoons garam masala

½ tablespoon ground turmeric

½ teaspoon ground coriander

¼ teaspoon ground cumin

Pinch of ground cinnamon

¼ teaspoon cayenne pepper

3 tablespoons unsalted butter

2 tablespoons tomato paste

2 teaspoons Worcestershire sauce

1 tablespoon honey

SOUP:

1 tablespoon canola oil

½ medium yellow onion, sliced

9 medium shiitake mushrooms, sliced

1 quart (4 cups) Chicken Broth (see page 14)

2 carrots, peeled and cut into bite-size pieces

¼ cup soy sauce

¼ cup mirin

1 pound udon noodles, cooked

1 scallion, both green and white parts diced

DUCK:

3 (7.5-ounce) boneless, skin-on duck breasts

1 tablespoon olive oil

1 teaspoon garlic powder

1 teaspoon ground ginger

1 teaspoon salt

1 tablespoon unsalted butter

Seems the duck did not survive in the wasteland. I have managed to catch a few radgulls, and while they're fairly emaciated and disfigured, if you substitute two radgulls for one duck breast, you should probably get enough meat for this recipe.

TO MAKE THE ROUX:

1. In a small bowl, combine the flour, garam masala, turmeric, coriander, cumin, cinnamon, and cayenne.

2. In a medium sauté pan or skillet over medium-high heat, melt the butter. Add the flour and spices to the melted butter. Stir together until the flour has absorbed all the butter. Stir in the tomato paste, Worcestershire sauce, and honey. Once everything is combined, turn off the heat and set aside.

Continued on next page

TO MAKE THE DUCK:

3. Rub the duck breasts with the olive oil, and season with the garlic powder, ground ginger, and salt.

4. In a large sauté pan or skillet over medium-high heat, melt the butter. Place the duck skin-side down in the pan and cook for 5 to 8 minutes, until the skin is crispy. Flip and cook for another 5 to 6 minutes for medium doneness, then remove from pan.

TO MAKE THE SOUP:

5. Heat the canola oil in a large pot over medium-high heat. Add the onion and mushrooms and cook until softened, about 5 minutes. Add the chicken broth and carrots. Bring to a boil, then reduce the heat to low. Place the lid slightly ajar and simmer for 30 minutes.

6. Take one-quarter of the roux and place it in a ladle filled with some of the soup. Use another spoon to mix the roux into the soup before adding to the pot. Repeat until all of the roux is added. Add the soy sauce and mirin. Let simmer for 5 minutes.

7. To serve, add udon noodles to a bowl. Top with the soup, a duck breast, and scallions, then serve.

XANDER

~~TURNIP~~ ROOT MISO SOUP

I WAS ABLE TO REPLACE THE "KOMBU" AND "BONITO" INGREDIENTS WITH TWO WINGS OF A BLOATFLY AND THE SHELL OF A FOG CRAWLER. THESE ADD A REAL KICK TO THE BROTH.

S.P.E.C.I.A.L:
+2 ENDURANCE
FOR 1 HOUR

DIFFICULTY:
EASY

PREP TIME:
15 MINUTES

COOK TIME:
45 MINUTES

SERVINGS:
4

PAIRS WELL WITH:
BRAISED DEATHCLAW
STEAK (PAGE 97)

4 cups cold water

1 piece kombu (dried kelp)

½ cup dried bonito flakes

3 dried shiitake mushrooms

½ medium turnip, thinly sliced ← *XANDER ROOT WORKS NICELY HERE INSTEAD.*

1 scallion, chopped

2 tablespoons white miso paste

1. Prepare the soup base by combining the water, kombu, and bonito flakes in a large pot over medium-high heat and bring to a simmer. Simmer for 3 minutes. Remove the kombu and add the mushrooms. Reduce the heat to low and simmer for an additional 30 minutes, then strain the broth. Broth can be stored in the refrigerator for up to 1 week.

2. To make the soup, place the shiitake broth in a large pot over medium-high heat and bring to a simmer. Add the turnips and cook for 2 to 3 minutes or until tender. Add the scallions and cook for 1 minute. Reduce the heat to low, whisk in the miso, and serve.

CHICKEN NOODLE SOUP

Due to its well-known medical applications, this recipe can be found in
The Vault-Tec™ Basic Manual of Medical Knowledge.

It's also in the Child of the Atom's official religious text, Healing the Nuclear Soul.

One 10-ounce young green jackfruit in
   brine, firm centers removed

1 teaspoon garlic powder

¼ teaspoon ground star anise

1 teaspoon paprika

½ teaspoon salt, plus more for seasoning

½ teaspoon pepper, plus more
   for seasoning

1 tablespoon canola oil

1 tablespoon unsalted butter

2 tablespoons chicken fat

2 medium carrots, peeled and diced

½ medium yellow onion, diced

3 celery ribs, diced

1 teaspoon dried thyme

3 quarts (12 cups) Chicken Broth (page 14)

3 ounces uncooked egg noodles

Cooked chicken breast, chopped
   (from Chicken Broth recipe)

1. In a large bowl, toss the jackfruit, garlic powder, star anise, paprika, salt, and pepper together. Heat the canola oil in a medium sauté pan or skillet over medium-high heat. Add the jackfruit and cook for 5 to 7 minutes, until tender. Shred the jackfruit and set aside. If jackfruit is difficult to shred, cook for a few minutes more to soften the fruit further.

2. Heat the butter and chicken fat in a large, deep pot over medium-high heat. Add the carrots, onion, and celery ribs and cook for about 8 minutes, until vegetables are starting to soften. Add the thyme, season to taste with salt and pepper, then cook for another 5 minutes, until the vegetables are soft.

3. Add the chicken broth. Increase the heat to high and bring to a boil. Taste the broth and season with additional salt and pepper to taste. Add the egg noodles and cook for 5 minutes. Add the chicken breast and jackfruit and cook for another 5 minutes until the meat is heated through, then serve.

TATO SOUP

Potatoes and tomatoes are the best ingredients to fortify everyone from vault dwellers to the vault elite!

Looks like the radiation did me a favor for once, as tatos are easy to grow and makes this dish easier to prep. Too bad they're mealy and look like dirt. Guess I can't win them all.

2 tablespoons olive oil

1 tablespoon salt

2 teaspoons pepper

½ large sweet potato, peeled and cut into 1-inch-thick slices

½ large russet potato, peeled and cut into 1-inch-thick slices

1 medium carrot, peeled and cut into 1-inch slices

3 whole tomatoes, each cut into 8 portions

> *Replace these ingredients with 5 tatos.*

4 tablespoons (½ stick) butter

½ cup diced yellow onion

¼ cup diced shallots

½ cup diced leeks

1 small fennel bulb, diced

1 teaspoon dried thyme

1 teaspoon dried sage

¼ teaspoon red pepper flakes

1 cup vegetable broth

1 cup coconut milk

Sliced scallions for garnishing

Crumbled feta cheese for garnishing

1. Preheat the oven to 400°F. Line two baking sheets with aluminum foil. In a large bowl, combine the olive oil, salt, and pepper. Toss the sliced sweet potatoes, russet potatoes, carrots, and tomatoes in the olive oil mixture. Spread the vegetables in one layer on the prepared baking sheets. Roast for 40 minutes. Set aside.

2. Melt the butter in a large, deep pot over medium heat. Add the onion, shallots, leeks, and fennel and cook until soft, 8 to 15 minutes. Sprinkle with the thyme, sage, and red pepper flakes. Add the roasted vegetables and vegetable broth and bring to a slight boil. Reduce the heat to low and simmer for 10 minutes.

3. Turn off the heat. Transfer the contents in the pot to a blender and blend until smooth. Return to the pot over low heat. Add the coconut milk and cook until the soup has warmed all the way through. Serve topped with scallions and feta cheese.

BRAHMIN
~~BEEF~~ AND VEGETABLE ROAST SOUP

THIS SOUP SEEMS TO BE EXTREMELY POPULAR IN SAN FRANCISCO CHINATOWN. THE LOCAL BRAHMIN HUNTERS SUGGESTED PUSHING THE BEAST OVER, SOMETHING CALLED BRAHMIN TIPPING, TO IMPROVE THE TENDERNESS OF THE MEAT. I CAN'T TELL IF THEY WERE BEING SARCASTIC OR JUST RUDE.

S.P.E.C.I.A.L:
+1 TO STRENGTH AND ENDURANCE FOR 4 HOURS

DIFFICULTY:
DIFFICULT

PREP TIME:
1 HOUR

COOK TIME:
4 TO 6 HOURS

SERVINGS:
5 OR 6

PAIRS WELL WITH:
RED WINE, CHEESE TOAST

BEEF RIBS:

3½ pounds ~~beef short ribs~~, BRAHMIN RIBS sliced into eight 3-inch portions

2 teaspoons salt

2 teaspoons freshly ground pepper

2 teaspoons ground cumin

1 teaspoon ground coriander

2 teaspoons garlic powder

½ teaspoon ground cardamom

¼ cup minced fresh ginger

Canola oil as needed

3 garlic cloves, minced

1 lemongrass stalk

1 cinnamon stick

1 small daikon radish, peeled, quartered and sliced in ½-inch pieces

1 small lotus root, quartered and sliced in ½-inch peeled pieces

1 medium carrot, peeled, halved, and sliced in ½-inch pieces

10 medium shiitake mushrooms, sliced

1 medium Asian pear, cut into bite-size peeled pieces

1 cup soy sauce

¾ cup rice wine vinegar

¼ cup sugar

BROTH:

1½ quarts (6 cups) beef broth

1 piece kombu (dried kelp)

2 bay leaves

1 lemongrass stalk

2 cups sauce from cooked braised ribs

1 cup rice noodles, cooked

Chopped scallions for garnishing

Bean sprouts for garnishing

A POT OF DIRTY WATER WILL SUBSTITUTE JUST FINE ONCE YOU BOIL IT. THE SEASONING'S ALREADY IN THERE!

1. Soak the beef short ribs in cold water for 15 minutes to remove any excess blood, then dry thoroughly with paper towels. In a small bowl, combine the salt, pepper, cumin, coriander, garlic powder, and cardamom. Season the meat generously and set aside any of the unused spice mix.

2. Preheat the oven to 250°F. Heat a dutch oven or another ovenproof pot over medium-high heat and add 2 tablespoons canola oil. Place 4 short ribs in the pot and cook each side until browned, about 2 to 3 minutes per side. Remove from heat and set aside. Repeat with additional canola oil and remaining short ribs.

Continued on next page

3. Add 1 tablespoon canola oil to the pot followed by the garlic, ginger, lemongrass, cinnamon, and any remaining spice mixture. Cook for about 3 minutes, until fragrant, then add the daikon, lotus root, and carrot and then cook for about 5 minutes. Add the meat and mix well. Finally, add the shiitake mushrooms and pear.

4. In a medium bowl, combine the soy sauce, rice wine vinegar, and sugar. Pour into the pot and coat ingredients with the sauce. Cover and place in the oven. Cook for at least 5 hours and up to 7 hours, stirring every 90 minutes. The longer the meat cooks, the more tender it will be.

MIGHT AS WELL COOK IT FOR THE FULL 7 HOURS WHILE YOU HEAL THAT LEG OF YOURS AFTER ALMOST GETTING TRAMPLED BY THE BRAHMIN YOU'RE CURRENTLY BRAISING!

5. Make the broth 30 minutes prior to the meat being done. First combine the beef broth, kombu, bay leaves, and lemongrass in a large pot over low heat. Allow the broth to lightly simmer.

6. Remove the short ribs from the oven then ladle 2 cups of sauce from the pot with the meat into the broth.

7. Divide the rice noodles between serving bowls. Place 1 to 2 pieces of short ribs in each bowl, followed by vegetables and broth. Top with scallions and bean sprouts and serve.

GOAT CURRY RADSTAG STEW

Vault-Tec™ is always paving the way for future innovations, and in our quest for the greatest recipe of all time, we pushed the spiciness of this dish to the limits of human taste. Like the best of scientists, we made an intern test the results. Don't worry, this is a shade cooler than our last experiment, and that intern learned a valuable lesson about workplace safety.

THE ORIGINAL RECIPE ASKS FOR GOAT OR LAMB, BUT THE ONLY G.O.A.T. I'VE SEEN IN THE WASTELAND IS THE GENERALIZED OCCUPATIONAL APTITUDE TEST. IT TOLD ME I WAS SUPPOSED TO BECOME THE DINER'S NEW FRY COOK, AND I NEVER FORGOT THE DIRECTIVE TO "HOLD THE MUSTARD, EXTRA PICKLES."

S.P.E.C.I.A.L:
+2 AGILITY FOR 2 HOURS

DIFFICULTY:
MEDIUM

PREP TIME:
30 MINUTES

COOK TIME:
45 MINUTES

SERVINGS:
6

PAIRS WELL WITH:
RICE

1 tablespoon canola oil

One 3-inch piece fresh ginger, peeled and grated

6 garlic cloves, chopped

1 lemongrass stalk, trimmed and chopped

2 medium red onions, sliced

1 tablespoon ground turmeric

2 tablespoons ground coriander

1 tablespoon ground cumin

2 tablespoons garam masala

1 teaspoon cayenne pepper

1 tablespoon ground fennel

2 teaspoons salt

1 serrano pepper, seeded and chopped

2 pounds goat or lamb meat, cut into bite-size pieces

One 28-ounce can chopped tomatoes

2 bay leaves

2 cups coconut milk

1 cup cilantro, measured then roughly chopped

Cooked white rice for serving

RADSTAG COMPLEMENTS THESE SPICES THE BEST, THOUGH "GAMY" IS PROBABLY THE NICEST WAY TO DESCRIBE THE MEAT.

1. Heat the canola oil in a large pot over medium-high heat. Add the garlic, ginger, and lemongrass and cook for 3 minutes, until fragrant. Add the red onion and cook until the onion just starts to brown, about 5 minutes more.

2. Mix in the turmeric, coriander, cumin, garam masala, cayenne, salt, and serrano pepper. Then add the goat meat and cook for 5 minutes, stirring occasionally to brown. Stir in the tomatoes and bay leaves. Reduce the heat to low, cover, and simmer for 15 minutes. Add the coconut milk and simmer for another 15 minutes, uncovered, until slightly thickened. Stir in the cilantro. Serve over rice.

CAROL'S MYSTERY MEAT STEW
VAULT-TEC'S MEATY CHILI

When I visited Carol's Place in the Capital Wasteland, Greta gave me some wonderful mystery meat to substitute into the chili. She couldn't tell me what it was, just that it was extremely fresh and a "family secret."

S.P.E.C.I.A.L:
+2 ENDURANCE
FOR 3 HOURS

DIFFICULTY:
MEDIUM

PREP TIME:
30 MINUTES

COOK TIME:
4 TO 7 HOURS

SERVINGS:
5 BOWLS OR
15 CHILI DOGS

PAIRS WELL WITH:
BLUE CORNBREAD
MUFFINS (PAGE 69)

1 whole fresh poblano pepper, seeds and stem removed

1 large yellow bell pepper, halved and seeded

1 large red bell pepper, halved and seeded

1 medium yellow onion, quartered

Olive oil for brushing

2 tablespoons canola oil

1 pound ground beef

1 pound ground lamb

2 teaspoons salt, plus more for seasoning

1 teaspoon pepper, plus more for seasoning

2½ tablespoons ground cumin

3 tablespoons chili powder

1 tablespoon brown sugar

2 tablespoons ground coffee

1 tablespoon ground fenugreek

2 teaspoons Worcestershire sauce

4 garlic cloves, minced

1 jalapeno, seeded and diced

One 15.5-ounce can red kidney beans

One 28-ounce can diced tomatoes

3 bay leaves

1. Preheat the oven to 450°F. Place the poblano pepper, bell peppers, and onion on a baking sheet. Brush with olive oil and season with salt and pepper. Bake for 30 to 40 minutes, until the peppers have softened and start to blacken. Remove from the oven and wrap in foil. Let rest for 30 minutes or until cool enough to work with. Remove the blackened pepper skin. Dice everything and set aside.

2. Heat the canola oil in a large, deep pot over medium heat. Add the beef and lamb and cook until browned. Add the salt, pepper, cumin, chili powder, brown sugar, ground coffee, fenugreek, and Worcestershire sauce, then mix until well combined. Add the garlic, jalapeno, and roasted vegetables. Stir in the kidney beans and diced tomatoes. Finally, add the bay leaves, cover, and reduce the heat to low.

3. Simmer for 4 to 6 hours. The longer you let it cook, the more the flavors will infuse. Remove the bay leaves before serving.

SIDES

BLAMCO MAC AND CHEESE

Thanks to our partnership with BlamCo, every vault is stocked with everyone's favorite BlamCo-brand mac and cheese. However, in case a mole rat infestation affects the boxes we've stockpiled, we've provided this recipe so you'll never be without your favorite dish!

1 pound elbow macaroni, cooked

2 medium carrots, chopped

1½ cups whole milk

½ cup heavy cream

2 teaspoons Worcestershire sauce

¼ cup all-purpose flour

2 teaspoons ground mustard

2 teaspoons garlic powder

¼ teaspoon cayenne pepper

5 tablespoons unsalted butter

8 ounces sharp cheddar cheese, shredded

4 ounces fontina cheese, shredded

Salt and pepper

I'VE MANAGED TO MASH UP AND RESHAPE SOME RAZORGRAIN INTO LUMPY CURVED PIECES OF DOUGH THAT WORK WELL ENOUGH AS PASTA IN THIS DISH.

S.P.E.C.I.A.L:
+1 AGILITY FOR 1 HOUR

DIFFICULTY:
EASY

PREP TIME:
30 MINUTES

COOK TIME:
30 MINUTES

SERVINGS:
5

PAIRS WELL WITH:
ROASTED VEGETABLES

1. Fill a medium pot with water and bring to a boil. Add the carrots, cover, reduce the heat to medium, and simmer for 5 minutes, or until the carrots are tender. Drain and transfer the carrots into a blender. Add the milk, heavy cream, and Worcestershire sauce. Blend until smooth.

2. Combine the flour, ground mustard, garlic powder, and cayenne pepper in a small bowl. Place a large saucepan over medium-high heat and add the butter. Once butter is melted, add the spiced flour while constantly whisking. After the butter and flour have combined into a roux, slowly whisk in the carrot and milk mixture until fully combined.

3. Whisk in the cheddar and fontina cheese in small batches. Season with salt and pepper. Add the cooked macaroni to the cheese sauce and stir to coat the macaroni fully.

I ONCE FOUND AN ACTUAL BOX OF BLAMCO MAC AND CHEESE IN AN ABANDONED HOUSE AND IT COOKED UP PERFECTLY. IT TASTED JUST LIKE IT DID WHEN I WAS A KID. SAY WHAT YOU WILL ABOUT CORPORATIONS FROM THE TIME AROUND THE GREAT WAR, THEY SURE KNEW HOW TO PRESERVE FOOD.

INSTAMASH

With its real dig-in flavor, InstaMash is a favorite of vault dwellers everywhere. Here you'll find our best imitation recipe. It's quick to make, but it's not *Insta*Mash.

1⅓ pounds russet potatoes, peeled and quartered

1 bay leaf

1 fresh rosemary sprig

1 teaspoon salt

¼ cup unsalted butter

¼ cup sour cream

½ cup crumbled blue cheese

1 teaspoon fresh parsley, minced then measured

Salt and pepper

I DON'T USUALLY INCLUDE BLUE CHEESE IN MY MASHED POTATOES, BUT IT CERTAINLY REMINDS ME OF INSTAMASH'S INSTANTLY RECOGNIZABLE WHITE AND BLUE BOX.

1. Fill a large pot with water and add the potatoes, bay leaf, rosemary sprig, and salt. Bring to a boil over high heat, then reduce the heat to medium and simmer for 15 to 20 minutes, until the potatoes are tender.

2. Drain the water and remove the bay leaf and rosemary sprig. Place the pot back on the stove over low heat and add the butter and sour cream. Mash the potatoes until smooth. Add the blue cheese and parsley and stir to combine. Season with salt and pepper to taste.

Blue **CORNBREAD MUFFINS**

Cornbread muffins are a staple of any delicious spread! Well-ground cornmeal is recommended for this recipe. If you can't find it in your bountifully stocked vault storage rooms, just place coarse cornmeal in a food processor and run until there are finer particles. Yellow cornmeal works in this recipe as well.

1¼ cups finely ground blue cornmeal

1 cup all-purpose flour

1 tablespoon baking powder

1 teaspoon salt

½ teaspoon ground turmeric

1 teaspoon ground cumin

2 teaspoons ground coriander

⅓ cup unsalted butter, melted and cooled

1 cup buttermilk

1 egg

½ cup sugar

¼ cup honey

CORN IS DELICIOUS AND I DON'T KNOW WHY MORE RECIPES DON'T USE IT! I SUPPOSE ITS ODD COLOR IS A LITTLE OFF-PUTTING, BUT I'VE COOKED UP MUCH STRANGER LOOKING THINGS.

S.P.E.C.I.A.L:
+1 LUCK FOR 30 MINUTES

DIFFICULTY:
EASY

PREP TIME:
15 MINUTES

COOK TIME:
30 MINUTES

SERVINGS:
12 TO 14 MUFFINS

PAIRS WELL WITH:
CAROL'S MYSTERY MEAT STEW (PAGE 61), RIBS

1. Preheat the oven to 400°F and line a muffin tin with paper liners.

2. Combine the cornmeal, flour, baking powder, salt, turmeric, cumin, and coriander in a large bowl. In another bowl, whisk together the butter, buttermilk, egg, sugar, and honey. Add the wet ingredients to the dry ingredients and mix until combined, but do not overmix.

3. Fill each muffin cup three-quarters of the way up with the batter. Bake for 12 to 15 minutes, until the tops are golden brown and a toothpick inserted into the center of a muffin comes out clean.

BAKED PORK N' BEANS

I'VE FOUND SO MANY PORK N' BEANS CANS WHILE WANDERING ACROSS THE WASTELAND, I HAVE AN ENTIRE HOARD OF THIS STUFF STASHED IN A RUSTED-OUT REFRIGERATOR. THIS RECIPE DEFINITELY HELPS CHANGE UP THE FLAVOR AFTER WEEKS OF JUST EATING OUT OF THE CAN.

1 teaspoon canola oil

8 bacon slices

½ medium yellow onion, diced

1 jalapeno, seeded and diced

3 garlic cloves, chopped

1 cup ketchup

½ cup brown sugar

½ cup honey

½ cup apple cider

1 tablespoon apple cider vinegar

1 teaspoon ground ginger

1 tablespoon ground mustard

1 tablespoon Worcestershire sauce

One 8.5-ounce can lima beans, drained and rinsed

Two 16-ounce cans pork and beans

Salt and pepper

I CAN SPOT A RUSTED-OUT RED AND BLUE CAN OF PORK N' BEANS FROM 50 YARDS AWAY.

S.P.E.C.I.A.L:
+1 AGILITY FOR 1 HOUR

DIFFICULTY:
EASY

PREP TIME:
30 MINUTES

COOK TIME:
1 HOUR 30 MINUTES

SERVINGS:
6

PAIRS WELL WITH:
DUSTY'S BRAHMIN BURGERS (PAGE 89)

1. Preheat the oven to 300°F. Heat the canola oil in a large dutch oven over medium-high heat. Add 4 slices of bacon and cook until crispy. Remove the bacon and drain on paper towels. Repeat with the remaining bacon.

2. Drain at least half of the bacon grease from the pan, then add the onions and cook until softened, about 5 minutes. Add the jalapeno and garlic and cook for 1 minute. Add the ketchup, brown sugar, honey, apple cider, apple cider vinegar, ground ginger, ground mustard, and Worcestershire sauce, and stir until well combined. Add the bacon back to the pot, stir, and bring to a simmer over low heat.

3. Add the beans and gently stir to combine. Transfer to the oven and bake, uncovered, for 45 to 50 minutes, until sauce is thickened. Season with salt and pepper.

BRAHMIN
~~TWICE~~-BAKED POTATOES

Baking a potato twice makes it twice as delicious!

SAUCE:

½ cup mayonnaise

¼ cup ketchup

1 tablespoon ground mustard

½ tablespoon Worcestershire sauce

1 teaspoon dried dill

2 teaspoons prepared horseradish

POTATOES:

2 large russet potatoes

3 tablespoons unsalted butter

2 ounces cream cheese

2 tablespoons sour cream

1 teaspoon caraway seed (optional)

Salt and pepper

1 cup prepared sauerkraut

1 cup prepared corned ~~beef~~ BRAHMIN

1 cup Swiss cheese, shredded

S.P.E.C.I.A.L:
+1 AGILITY FOR 30
MINUTES

DIFFICULTY:
EASY

PREP TIME:
30 MINUTES

COOK TIME:
1 HOUR 30 MINUTES

SERVINGS:
4

PAIRS WELL WITH:
SADDLE UP SALISBURY
STEAK (PAGE 109),
DUSTY'S BRAHMIN
BURGERS (PAGE 89)

1. Make the sauce in a small bowl by stirring all of the sauce ingredients together. Set aside.

2. Preheat the oven to 400°F. Wash and dry the potatoes. Pierce each potato several times with a fork and place on a baking sheet. Bake for 1 hour or until tender. Remove from the oven and reduce the heat to 350°F. Allow to cool.

3. When the potatoes are cool enough to handle, cut them in half lengthwise. Carefully scoop out the potato flesh into a separate bowl while leaving a ¼-inch-thick wall in the potato. Do not tear the potato shell.

4. Place the butter, cream cheese, and sour cream in a large pot over medium heat. Allow the butter to melt slightly, then add the potato flesh and mash until smooth. Turn off the heat. Stir in the caraway seeds if using and season with salt and pepper. Set aside.

5. In each potato skin, add 2 dollops of the sauce. Place a spoonful of the mashed potatoes in each of the potato skins. Top each filled potato with sauerkraut, corned beef, and Swiss cheese. Bake for 15 minutes. Turn on the broiler and cook until the cheese begins to brown, about 2 to 3 minutes.

SUGAR-BOMBED CARROTS

Having a hard time getting the kids to eat their vegetables? Look no further than our delicious recipe for Sugar-Bombed Carrots! These carrots, and your kids, will be hit with so much sugar, they won't know what to do with it all!

2 pounds carrots, peeled and sliced

¼ cup sugar

1 tablespoon maple syrup

4 tablespoons (½ stick) unsalted butter, divided

2 teaspoons salt, divided

⅓ cup coconut milk

⅓ cup brown sugar

⅔ cup Sugar Bombs or other sugar-frosted flake cereal

¼ cup chopped walnuts

2 tablespoons candied ginger, diced

PRE-WAR CARROTS MUST HAVE BEEN SO TIME-CONSUMING TO PEEL CONSIDERING HOW THIN THEY WERE, AND WITH ONLY ONE ROOT!

S.P.E.C.I.A.L:
+2 PERCEPTION
FOR 30 MINUTES

DIFFICULTY:
EASY

PREP TIME:
30 MINUTES

COOK TIME:
1 HOUR 30 MINUTES

SERVINGS:
4

PAIRS WELL WITH:
THE CAPTAIN'S
FEAST (PAGE 107)

1. Preheat the oven to 350°F. Bring a large pot of water to a boil over high heat and add the carrots. Reduce the heat to medium-low and simmer for 30 to 40 minutes, until very tender. Drain the carrots. Place the carrots, sugar, maple syrup, 2 tablespoons of the butter, and 1 teaspoon of the salt in a large bowl and mash until smooth. Add the coconut milk and stir to combine. Transfer to a 9-by-12 baking dish.

2. Combine the brown sugar, cereal, walnuts, remaining 2 tablespoons butter, remaining 1 teaspoon salt, and candied ginger in a food processor and pulse lightly until it forms a crumbly texture. Top the mashed carrots with the crumble.

3. Bake, uncovered, for 30 minutes. Turn on the broiler and heat for 5 minutes, until crispy.

PIPER'S SPECIAL **SODA BREAD**

On my visit to Diamond City, I ran into an enterprising journalist named Piper. She requested an interview after hearing I was a vault dweller so I happily obliged. She was so thankful for all of the material I gave her for a new article that she shared her family's secret soda bread ingredient: dried mutfruit!

4 cups all-purpose flour

½ cup sugar

1 teaspoon salt

1 tablespoon baking powder

1 teaspoon baking soda

6 tablespoons (¾ stick) unsalted butter, cubed,
   at room temperature, plus more for greasing the pan

1 cup raisins

½ cup dried cranberries ← SUBSTITUTE THE SAME AMOUNT OF IRRADIATED MUTFRUIT THAT'S BEEN LEFT TO DRY OUT IN THE SUN.

1½ cups buttermilk

1 egg

S.P.E.C.I.A.L:
+1 PERCEPTION
FOR 1 HOUR

DIFFICULTY:
EASY

PREP TIME:
30 MINUTES

COOK TIME:
1 HOUR 15 MINUTES

SERVINGS:
1 LOAF

PAIRS WELL WITH:
BUTTER AND HONEY

1. Preheat the oven to 350°F. Combine the flour, sugar, salt, baking powder, and baking soda in a food processor or stand mixer fitted with the paddle attachment. Add the butter and pulse or mix on low until it resembles coarse meal, then transfer to a large bowl. Add the raisins and dried cranberries, then stir to combine.

2. Whisk the buttermilk and eggs in a small bowl. Add the buttermilk mixture to the large bowl and stir together with a spatula until just combined. The dough will still be wet.

3. Grease a 9-inch cake pan with additional butter. Place the dough in the prepared cake pan. With a sharp knife, make an X across the top of the dough. Bake for 1 hour, until a toothpick inserted into the center comes out clean. Cool completely.

BROCCOLI AND MUSHROOM CASSEROLE

Absent any major radiation event, the seeds stored in each carefully stocked vault should provide a wide variety of produce—including broccoli—far into the future.

I spoke with Janice Kaplinski at Rivet City for a bit about her research into nutrition and health. She had studied extinct vegetables but had never seen broccoli before, though she thought she might be able to grow some soon. I guess I'll have to wait until she's successful to try out this recipe.

I'll probably use cave mushrooms instead.

2 heads broccoli, halved

3 tablespoons unsalted butter

½ medium yellow onion, chopped

4 garlic cloves, minced

10 shiitake mushrooms, chopped

10 button mushrooms, chopped

2 tablespoons all-purpose flour

1 teaspoon dried thyme

2 teaspoons dried basil

1 cup coconut milk

½ cup vegetable broth

1 cup shredded fontina cheese

1½ cups rice, cooked

1 cup shredded mozzarella

S.P.E.C.I.A.L:
+1 STRENGTH
FOR 30 MINUTES

DIFFICULTY:
MEDIUM

PREP TIME:
30 MINUTES

COOK TIME:
40 MINUTES

SERVINGS:
6

PAIRS WELL WITH:
MIRELURK QUEEN
STEAK (PAGE 91)

1. Preheat oven to 425°F degrees. Fit a large pot with a steamer basket over medium-high heat and bring 1 inch of water to boil. Place the broccoli in the steamer basket and steam for 10 minutes. Remove the broccoli, roughly chop it, and set it aside.

2. In a large sauté pan or skillet over medium-high heat, melt the butter. Add the onion and garlic and cook for 2 minutes, until the onion is slightly transparent. Add the shiitake and button mushrooms and cook until tender, about 8 to 10 minutes. Add the flour, thyme, and basil, making sure to incorporate the flour fully. Whisk in the coconut milk and vegetable broth. Add the broccoli. Add the fontina cheese and stir until melted. Finally, fold in the rice.

3. Transfer to a 9-by-13-inch baking dish. Top with mozzarella cheese and bake for 18 minutes, until the cheese turns golden brown.

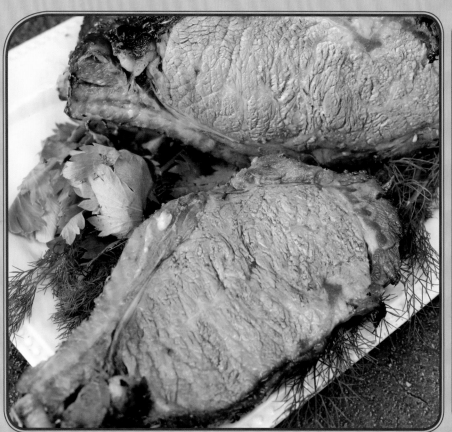

MAINS

BAKED BLOATFLY VEGETARIAN MEATLOAF

Vault dwellers will not be exposed to sunlight while living in our spacious vaults, but this vegetarian meatloaf will supply everyone with all of the necessary nutrition, including vitamin D.

I RAN OUT OF RATIONS ON ONE OF MY RECENT OUTINGS INTO THE WASTELAND AND HAD TO RESORT TO SOME UNORTHODOX FOOD PREP. I CAUGHT A FEW BLOATFLIES, ROASTED THEM UP, AND MANAGED TO GET IT ALL DOWN. I THINK I'LL HAVE TO SWITCH TO VEGETARIAN MEALS LIKE THIS ONE FOR A WHILE TO GET THE TASTE OUT OF MY MOUTH, BUT THE TEXTURE OF THIS RECIPE STILL HAS A NICE CRUNCH TO IT.

S.P.E.C.I.A.L:
+2 STRENGTH
FOR 2 HOURS

DIFFICULTY:
MEDIUM

PREP TIME:
45 MINUTES

COOK TIME:
2 HOURS

SERVINGS:
4

PAIRS WELL WITH:
SUGAR-BOMBED CARROTS (PAGE 75)

2 tablespoons olive oil

1 portobello mushroom, chopped

3 button mushrooms, chopped

2 shiitake mushrooms, chopped

1 medium yellow onion, chopped

1 orange bell pepper, chopped

¼ bunch cilantro, chopped

3 tablespoons fresh tarragon, chopped then measured

4 teaspoons dried basil

3 tablespoons fresh sage, chopped then measured

¾ cup cashews

½ cup walnuts

One 15-ounce can chickpeas, drained

½ cup cooked quinoa

½ cup panko bread crumbs

2½ tablespoons ketchup

2 tablespoons steak sauce

1 teaspoon liquid smoke (optional)

Salt and pepper

⅓ cup Nuka-Cola BBQ Sauce (page 15)

1. Preheat the oven to 375°F. Line a loaf pan with parchment paper. Make sure the parchment paper is hanging out of the pan so it will be easier to pull the loaf out of the pan when it's done.

2. Heat a large sauté pan or skillet over medium-high heat and spray with nonstick spray. Add the portobello, button, and shiitake mushrooms, onion, and peppers. Cook for about 10 minutes, until all the onions are translucent and the mushrooms are soft. Add the cilantro, tarragon, basil, and sage. Cook for 5 minutes. Remove from the heat and set aside.

Continued on next page

3. Place the cashews and walnuts in a food processor and pulse until crushed (do not overprocess). Transfer to a large bowl. Add the chickpeas to the food processor and pulse until smooth. Transfer to the bowl with the nuts. Add the cooked quinoa and panko. Stir until combined.

4. Take the sautéed vegetables and drain any liquid that may have settled in the pan. Add the vegetables to the large bowl and fold in with the rest of the items. Add the ketchup, steak sauce, and liquid smoke. Season with salt and pepper.

5. Transfer the vegetable mixture into the loaf pan. Make sure to press the mixture down tightly. Top the loaf with the Nuka-Cola BBQ Sauce. Bake for 1 hour.

6. Remove from the oven and let sit for 10 minutes. Line a baking sheet with parchment paper. Transfer the vegetable loaf from the loaf pan to a cutting board. Carefully cut into 1-inch-thick pieces. Be gentle, because the loaf will be a bit soft and can crumble easily. Place the slices onto the prepared baking sheet and bake for 15 minutes, until the edges look slightly crispy. Remove from the oven and let sit for 10 minutes before serving, or longer if you prefer a firmer slice.

JOE'S SPUCKIES MEATBALL SPUCKIE

Craving one of Joe's famous meatball spuckies? Our scientists have replicated and, dare I say, improved upon his iconic recipe so that you can enjoy the classic South Boston treat whenever you want! If you can't find veal, replace it with more beef or turkey.

S.P.E.C.I.A.L:
+2 ENDURANCE
FOR 3 HOURS

DIFFICULTY:
MEDIUM

PREP TIME:
1 HOUR

COOK TIME:
30 MINUTES

SERVINGS:
24 SLIDERS

PAIRS WELL WITH:
NUKA-COLA (PAGE 165)

1 pound ground beef

10 ounces ground veal

7 ounces ground turkey

2 eggs yolks

1 cup grated Parmesan cheese

1 medium carrot, shredded

½ medium yellow onion, minced

8 garlic cloves, minced

½ cup panko bread crumbs

2 tablespoons dried basil

1 teaspoon ground fennel seed

2 teaspoons chili powder

2 teaspoons salt

1 teaspoon pepper

5 tablespoons dried oregano, divided

2 tablespoons canola oil

32 ounces prepared marinara sauce

24 thin slices fresh mozzarella (optional)

4 tablespoons (½ stick) unsalted butter, melted

2 teaspoons garlic powder

6 hoagie rolls

1. Mix the beef, veal, turkey, and egg yolks in a large bowl with your hands until smooth. Add the Parmesan cheese, carrot, onion, and garlic to the meat and mix to incorporate. Finally, add the panko, basil, fennel, chili powder, salt, pepper, and 3 tablespoons of the oregano, and stir until all ingredients have melded together. Roll the meat into 24 equal portions.

2. Heat two large sauté pans or skillets with 1 tablespoon of canola oil each over medium-high heat. Fry the meatballs for about 10 to 15 minutes, turning so they are browned on all sides. Pour the marinara sauce over the browned patties. Reduce the heat to medium-low, cover, and simmer for 20 minutes, until meatballs are cooked through. Turn off the heat.

3. If using mozzarella, top each meatball with a piece of fresh mozzarella, and cover again for another two minutes to let the cheese melt.

4. Combine the melted butter, garlic powder, and remaining 2 tablespoons of oregano in a small bowl, then brush on the insides of the rolls and toast under a broiler until golden brown. Spoon a few of the meatballs into each roll and serve.

DUSTY'S BRAHMIN
BISON BURGERS

Every great American cook should know how to make a great American burger. It is our duty to set out into the wild unknown and tame mother nature's greatest hurdles, so we thought a bison burger would help drive that proud pioneering spirit once again as soon as the all-clear is given at your vault.

1 pound ground bison or ground beef

2 round onion slices

Olive oil

4 pretzel buns

4 slices cheddar cheese

Nuka-Cola BBQ Sauce (see page 15)

4 butter lettuce leaves

4 tomato slices

Mayonnaise for serving

Salt and pepper

I HAVEN'T FOUND ANY BISON—NO SURPRISE—BUT DUSTY OVER AT NCR DOWNTOWN SWEARS UP AND DOWN ON THE DELICIOUS TASTE OF BRAHMIN.

S.P.E.C.I.A.L:
+2 AGILITY
FOR 30 MINUTES

DIFFICULTY:
EASY

PREP TIME:
15 MINUTES

COOK TIME:
10 MINUTES

SERVINGS:
4

PAIRS WELL WITH:
NUKA-COLA (PAGE 165),
FRIED POTATOES

TO MAKE THE BURGERS:

1. Preheat a grill. In a large bowl, mix the ground bison with a generous amount of salt and pepper and divide into 4 equal portions. Shape the meat into patties slightly larger than the buns you are using.

2. Rub the onion slices with olive oil and season with salt and pepper. Place the onion near the main source of heat on the grill. Cook until nearly charred. Transfer to a plate and cover with aluminum foil.

3. Place the bison patties over the main source of heat on the grill. Cook each side for 4 minutes. Add slices of cheese on the patties, cover the grill, and cook for 1 minute to melt the cheese.

TO ASSEMBLE:

4. Take the bottom portion of a bun and add a large amount of the Nuka-Cola BBQ Sauce. Add a slice of butter lettuce and top with a portion of the onions. Place the bison patty and tomato slice. Spread mayo on the top bun and place on top.

MIRELURK QUEEN STEAK
CRAB-STUFFED SALMON

As scientists, we sometimes spend too much time devising ways to take things apart and put them back together. Thanks to the wonders of modern food science, we have discovered that the more tasty food items you can shove into each other, the tastier the results will be.

S.P.E.C.I.A.L:
+2 ENDURANCE
FOR 1 HOUR

DIFFICULTY:
EASY

PREP TIME:
20 MINUTES

COOK TIME:
30 MINUTES

SERVINGS:
2

PAIRS WELL WITH:
GREEN SIDE SALAD

½ tablespoon canola oil

2 scallions, green and white parts sliced

3 white mushrooms, sliced

½ cup spinach, measured then chopped

½ cup lump crabmeat ←

½ cup cream cheese, at room temperature

3 teaspoons lemon juice

½ teaspoon celery salt

Two 4-ounce salmon fillets

Salt and pepper

IT SEEMS THE BELLY OF THE MIRELURK QUEEN AND ITS CLAWS MAKE FOR A GREAT REPLACEMENT IN THIS RECIPE. JUST BE CAREFUL WHEN FIGHTING ONE!

1. Preheat the oven to 350°F. Line a baking sheet with foil.

2. Heat the canola oil in a medium sauté pan or skillet over medium-high heat. Add the scallions and mushrooms and cook until softened, about 5 minutes. Add the spinach and cook until the spinach has wilted, about 2 minutes. Remove from the heat and let cool. Once cool, squeeze the vegetables to remove any remaining liquid.

3. Combine the cooked veggies, crabmeat, cream cheese, lemon juice, and celery salt in a small bowl. Place the salmon fillets on the prepared baking sheet and season with salt and pepper. Make a small incision lengthwise along each fillet, but do not slice all the way through. Divide the crabmeat mixture in half and stuff into the incisions, and pile additional stuffing on top of the filet. Bake for 18 to 20 minutes, until the stuffing just begins to brown.

POACHED ~~COD~~ ANGLER

Fishing is a bit like science, in a way. We peer into the great unknown, unsure what lies below the surface, with only our tools and our ingenuity to search the secrets the depths hold. And sometimes we find something delicious. Metaphorically, of course.

COD WERE SUPPOSEDLY WELL-MANNERED, MILD-TASTING FISH. ANGLERS ARE QUITE AGGRESSIVE, BUT THEIR SIMPLE TASTE AND TEXTURE MUST BE CLOSE, AND THE BIOLUMINESCENT GROWTH ON ITS HEAD MAKES A GREAT GARNISH.

S.P.E.C.I.A.L:
+2 PERCEPTION
FOR 2 HOURS

DIFFICULTY:
EASY

PREP TIME:
30 MINUTES

COOK TIME:
30 MINUTES

SERVINGS:
5

PAIRS WELL WITH:
ROASTED POTATOES

1 tablespoon canola oil

One 2-inch piece fresh ginger, peeled and minced

1 lemongrass stalk

4 garlic cloves, minced

1½ cups vegetable broth

1 teaspoon lime zest

2½ cups coconut milk

1 tablespoon fish sauce

1 pound boneless, skinless cod, cut into 5 pieces

3 baby bok choy, quartered

5 shiitake mushrooms, stemmed and sliced

2 tablespoons lime juice

Salt and pepper

1. Heat the canola oil in a large pot over medium-high heat. Add the ginger, lemongrass, and garlic, then cook for 5 minutes. Add the vegetable broth and lime zest. Bring to a slight boil, reduce the heat to medium, and allow the broth to simmer for 10 minutes. Remove the lemongrass. Add the coconut milk and fish sauce and stir well.

2. Season the cod with salt and pepper. Add the cod to the pot and bring to a simmer. The cod does not need to be fully submerged. Cover and cook for 5 minutes. The internal temperature of the fish should reach 140°F. Remove the cod and place on a serving plate.

3. Add the bok choy and mushrooms to the broth and cook until wilted, about 3 minutes. Add the vegetables to the plate with the cod. Turn off the heat and stir in the lime juice. Ladle the broth over the cod.

SPILED ~~CRAB LEGS~~

Vault-Tec™ has provided a cryogenic freezer to make sure every vault dweller will be able to freeze and unfreeze meat whenever they like, providing the freshest ingredients for years to come.

UPDATE: CRYOGENIC CHAMBERS WERE MADE TO FREEZE LARGE AMOUNTS OF FOOD. PLEASE DISREGARD ANY RUMORS THAT ALLEGE THEY ARE SIZED FOR HUMAN BEINGS.

S.P.E.C.I.A.L:
+2 LUCK
FOR 15 MINUTES

DIFFICULTY:
MEDIUM

PREP TIME:
15 MINUTES

COOK TIME:
20 MINUTES

SERVINGS:
4

PAIRS WELL WITH:
WHITE RICE,
BUTTER SAUCE

4 snow crab leg clusters

⅓ cup ketchup

⅓ cup soy sauce

2 tablespoons oyster sauce

1 tablespoon fish sauce

¼ cup sambal chili paste

2 tablespoons brown sugar

1 cup chicken broth

2 tablespoons canola oil

1 medium shallot, minced

8 garlic cloves, minced

One 1-inch piece fresh ginger, peeled and minced

1 lemongrass stalk, minced

1 jalapeno, minced

2 tablespoons cornstarch

2 tablespoons water

Sliced scallions for garnishing

Fresh chopped cilantro for garnishing

IT'S EASY TO SUBSTITUTE IN ONE MIRELURK CLAW FOR TWO CRAB LEG CLUSTERS. I SUGGEST SHOOTING THE MIRELURKS IN THE FACE SO YOU DON'T HAVE TO PICK SHRAPNEL AND BUCKSHOT OUT OF THE MEATY CLAWS.

1. Cut and crack the crab legs between each of the leg sections so the sauce will be able to reach the meat. Do not remove the shells.

2. In a medium bowl, combine the ketchup, soy sauce, oyster sauce, fish sauce, sambal chili paste, brown sugar, and chicken broth. Heat the canola oil in a large pot with a lid over medium-high heat. Add the shallots, garlic, ginger, lemongrass, and jalapeno, and cook until fragrant, about 5 to 8 minutes. Stir in the ketchup mixture and allow to heat up.

3. In a small bowl, combine the water and cornstarch, then add to the pot and stir until thickened.

4. Add the cracked crab legs, cover the pot, and shake to cover the legs. Cook for 5 minutes. Shake the pot again to make sure the legs are covered. Serve with scallions and cilantro.

BRAISED ~~PORK BELLY~~

Regularly study your Vault-Tec™—provided materials, because an empty mind is an empty vessel, waiting to be filled—just like an empty stomach is an empty vessel, waiting to be filled with this delicious braised meat.

I SAW THIS RECIPE AND KNEW RIGHT AWAY THAT DEATHCLAW MEAT WOULD WORK PERFECTLY WITH THE INGREDIENTS. DEATHCLAW MEAT IS JUST SO VERSATILE, THANKS TO THE NUMBER OF ANIMALS THAT WERE GENETICALLY ENGINEERED TOGETHER TO CREATE THESE MONSTROSITIES.

2¼ pounds 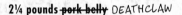 ~~pork belly~~ DEATHCLAW

1 tablespoon granulated sugar

2 tablespoons light brown sugar

⅓ cup water

1 cup sake

1 cup soy sauce

2 tablespoons rice vinegar

3 tablespoons hoisin sauce

1½ cups chicken broth

One 3-inch piece fresh ginger, peeled

3 garlic cloves

2 lemongrass stalks

3 bay leaves

3 star anise

3 cardamom pods

1 cinnamon stick

2 dried chiles de arbol (or other peppers such as cayenne)

1 tablespoon peppercorns

S.P.E.C.I.A.L:
+1 AGILITY FOR 1 HOUR

DIFFICULTY:
MEDIUM

PREP TIME:
30 MINUTES

COOK TIME:
2 HOURS

SERVINGS:
4 TO 6

PAIRS WELL WITH:
WHITE RICE,
STIR-FRIED VEGETABLES

1. Preheat the oven to 325°F. Place the pork belly in a large pot and cover with cold water over medium-high heat. Bring to a boil, then reduce the heat to medium-low and simmer for 15 minutes. Remove any foam that floats to the top. Remove the pork belly from the water and carefully cut into bite-size pieces.

2. Add the granulated sugar, light brown sugar, and ⅓ cup water to a large, ovenproof pot and place over medium-high heat. Whisk together until the sugar has dissolved, then add the pork belly to the pot and stir to coat. Add all the remaining ingredients to the pot and bring to a low boil.

3. Cover the pot with an ovenproof lid and transfer to the oven. Bake for 1 hour. Increase the heat of the oven to 375°F and remove the cover. Bake for 1 hour more, stirring the contents every 15 minutes.

4. Remove the pot from the oven and let it rest on the stove. Take a cup of the sauce from the pot and pour it into a small saucepan over high heat. Cook until the sauce reduces and thickens. Toss the pork pieces in the reduced sauce and serve.

RADSCORPION
~~CHICKEN~~ EN CROÛTE

We've all heard that so many things taste like chicken. If you ask us, chicken needs to learn its place. Where does chicken get off, having a monopoly on our taste buds? The center stage in our culinary theater? We've toiled and struggled to find an iconic flavor that can usurp chicken's crown, but alas, science can only go so far. Perhaps it is best we allow chicken to take its rightful place at the dinner table.

WHEN I VISITED MOM'S DINER, I COULDN'T BELIEVE HOW MUCH RADSCORPION TASTED LIKE CHICKEN. IT'S CERTAINLY EASIER TO FIND!

S.P.E.C.I.A.L:
+1 CHARISMA
FOR 1 HOUR

DIFFICULTY:
MEDIUM

PREP TIME:
30 MINUTES

COOK TIME:
1 HOUR

SERVINGS:
12

PAIRS WELL WITH:
SIDE SALAD,
ROASTED VEGETABLES

1 tablespoon unsalted butter

2 medium shallots, finely diced

2 scallions, green and white parts chopped

One 14-ounce can artichoke hearts, roughly chopped

8 ounces cream cheese

¼ cup grated Parmesan cheese

1 teaspoon ground fennel

½ tablespoon dried oregano

1 pound chicken breast tenders, pounded
   thin and cut into 12 pieces

2 sheets frozen puff pastry, thawed, rolled out,
   and cut into 12 equal pieces

Salt and pepper

1. Preheat the oven to 375°F. In a large sauté pan or skillet over medium-high heat, melt the butter. Add the shallots and scallions and cook for 5 minutes, until fragrant. Add the artichoke hearts and cook for another 5 minutes, until everything has warmed through. Remove from the heat and drain any liquid.

2. In a large bowl, combine the artichoke heart mixture with the cream cheese and Parmesan cheese. Stir well. Season with salt and pepper.

3. Combine the fennel and oregano in a small bowl. Season the chicken tenders with the spices. Roll out a piece of puff pastry and place a piece of chicken on top. Top with the artichoke and cream cheese mixture and roll up lengthwise. Place in a muffin tin vertically. Repeat with the remaining portions. Place in the oven and bake until the puff pastry is golden brown, about 50 minutes. Remove from the oven and cool for 10 minutes before removing from the muffin tin and serving.

DEATHCLAW WELLINGHAM
PORK POT PIES

After a bit of legwork and persuading, I managed to get some cooking secrets out of Wellingham over at Diamond City to adapt this recipe. He made me promise that I would only make it for elite individuals, but everyone is equally important in my kitchen.

The amount of meat behind a deathclaw's shoulder makes it tender and perfect for stewing and a great substitute here.

S.P.E.C.I.A.L:
+2 INTELLIGENCE
FOR 1 HOUR

DIFFICULTY:
MEDIUM

PREP TIME:
1 HOUR

COOK TIME:
1 HOUR 30 MINUTES

SERVINGS:
5

PAIRS WELL WITH:
BROCCOLI

2½ pounds boneless pork shoulder, cubed

¼ cup all-purpose flour

1 teaspoon salt

1 teaspoon pepper

3 tablespoons canola oil

2 celery ribs, chopped

2 medium carrots, peeled and chopped

1 medium yellow onion, chopped

1 leek, chopped

3 garlic cloves, minced

1 teaspoon dried rosemary

½ teaspoon caraway seeds

¼ cup vodka

2 tablespoons tomato paste

1 cup (4 cups) chicken broth

1 russet potato, peeled and cut into bite-size pieces

2 bay leaves

2 cups mushrooms, quartered

¼ cup cornstarch

½ cup water

2 sheets frozen puff pastry, cut in circles to cover bowls

1 egg yolk, beaten

Mutated fern flower spices up this recipe just right, and a tato can sub in for the vegetables as well.

If you manage to take down a deathclaw, see if you can find a deathclaw nest nearby for some delicious eggs.

1. In a large zip-top bag, toss the pork, flour, salt, and pepper together. Heat a dutch oven over medium-high heat with 2 tablespoons of the canola oil. Once warmed, place half of the pork in a single layer and cook. Cook each side until browned, about 2 to 3 minutes per side. Transfer to a plate, and repeat with the remaining pork.

2. Add another tablespoon of canola oil to the dutch oven. Add the celery, carrots, onion, leek, garlic, rosemary, and caraway seeds, and cook until the vegetables have softened. Deglaze the pan with the vodka, stirring to loosen any brown bits. Add the tomato paste and stir to combine. Add the chicken broth, potato, bay leaves, and pork. Bring to a boil and then reduce heat to medium-low, cover, and let simmer for 30 minutes. Add the mushrooms and simmer for about 15 minutes, until all the vegetables are tender.

3. Remove the bay leaves from the stew. In a small bowl, whisk together the cornstarch and water. Stir into the pork stew and cook until it thickens slightly. Remove from the heat and season with salt and pepper.

4. Preheat the oven to 400°F. Ladle portions of the stew into ovenproof ramekins or bowls. Top each with a round piece of puff pastry. Brush the tops with the beaten egg yolk and bake for about 15 minutes, until the crust is golden brown.

MOLE RAT
SAUSAGE MANICOTTI

MOM OVER AT MOM'S DINER LOVED THIS RECIPE, BUT THOUGHT MOLE RAT WOULD WORK JUST FINE AS A REPLACEMENT. WE ALSO DETERMINED THAT A COMBINATION OF HUBFLOWER AND A FEW FERN FLOWERS REPLACED THE SPICES EASILY. WELL, IT PROBABLY ISN'T NEARLY AS DELICIOUS BUT AT LEAST THE RECIPE WON'T TASTE LIKE DIRT.

S.P.E.C.I.A.L:
+1 INTELLIGENCE
FOR 1 HOUR

DIFFICULTY:
HARD

PREP TIME:
1 HOUR

COOK TIME:
1 HOUR

SERVINGS:
7

PAIRS WELL WITH:
FRENCH BREAD

2 ounces (25 grams) fresh basil

⅓ cup grated Parmesan cheese

¼ cup pine nuts

6 garlic cloves

¼ cup olive oil

½ cup soft goat cheese

3½ cups ricotta cheese

¼ cup parsley, measured and then chopped

1 tablespoon dried oregano

3 Italian sausages, removed from their casings, cooked, and roughly chopped

1 tablespoon unsalted butter

½ cup cream cheese

4 cups prepared marinara sauce, divided

1 cup shredded fontina cheese

¼ cup heavy cream

2 cups shredded mozzarella

14 manicotti noodles, cooked al dente

Salt and pepper

REPLACE WITH MOLE RAT, GROUND AND CHOPPED.

1. Combine the basil, Parmesan cheese, pine nuts, garlic, and olive oil in a food processor and pulse until smooth. Add the goat cheese and ricotta cheese and pulse until combined. Transfer to a medium bowl. Add the parsley, oregano, and cooked Italian sausage and stir to combine. Season with salt and pepper. Set aside.

2. Place a large saucepan over medium-high heat and add the butter and cream cheese. Heat until the butter has melted and the cream cheese has softened. Pour half of the marinara sauce into the pot and mix together until well combined. Add the fontina and heavy cream and heat until the cheese melts. Add the remaining marinara and simmer for 10 minutes. Season with salt and pepper. Turn off the heat and set aside.

3. Preheat the oven to 350°F. In a deep 9-by-13-inch baking dish, spread 1 cup of the sauce along the bottom. Carefully fill the manicotti with the sausage filling. Lay the filled manicotti in the baking tray in a single layer. Pour the remaining sauce over the manicotti, then top with shredded mozzarella. Bake, uncovered, for 30 to 45 minutes, until the cheese is bubbly.

MUTANT MANTIS
CHICKEN MARSALA

> I HAD A FANTASTIC PLATE OF MANTIS MARSALA AT MOM'S DINER, BUT I'VE BEEN HAVING A TOUGH TIME FINDING MANTIS LATELY. I'LL NEED TO PICK ANOTHER MUTANT CREATURE THAT MATCHES THE MANTIS'S EXOTIC TASTE.

S.P.E.C.I.A.L:
+1 INTELLIGENCE
FOR 2 HOURS

DIFFICULTY:
EASY

PREP TIME:
30 MINUTES

COOK TIME:
30 MINUTES

SERVINGS:
8

PAIRS WELL WITH:
ROASTED ASPARAGUS,
INSTAMASH (PAGE 67)

3 (6-ounce) boneless, skinless chicken breasts

⅔ cup all-purpose flour

⅓ cup cornstarch

1 teaspoon black pepper

1 teaspoon salt

½ teaspoon cayenne pepper

2 teaspoons dried thyme

3 tablespoons canola oil, divided

3 medium shallots, diced

1 leek, white and light green parts diced

3 garlic cloves, minced

4 ounces button mushrooms, stemmed and sliced

7 ounces baby portobello mushrooms, stemmed and sliced

5 ounces shiitake mushrooms, stemmed and sliced

3 dried apricots, thinly sliced

1 cup sweet marsala wine

1 cup chicken broth

1 teaspoon balsamic vinegar

1. Place a chicken breast between two pieces of plastic wrap and use a meat tenderizer to flatten to ½-inch thickness. Repeat with the remaining chicken breasts. *GET OUT THAT AGGRESSION!*

2. On a plate, combine the flour, cornstarch, black pepper, salt, cayenne pepper, and thyme.

3. Heat 2 tablespoons of the canola oil in a large sauté pan or skillet over medium-high heat. Dredge a chicken breast in the flour mixture and shake any excess off. Place in the hot pan and pan-fry until both sides of the chicken breast are golden brown, about 5 minutes per side. Remove the chicken and place on a plate. Repeat with the remaining chicken breasts.

4. When all of the chicken is cooked, add the remaining 1 tablespoon canola oil to the pan, along with the shallots, leek, and garlic. Sauté for about 3 minutes, until fragrant and lightly browned. Add the button, portobello, and shiitake mushrooms and cook until they have slightly browned, about 10 minutes. Add the dried apricot. Deglaze the pan with the sweet marsala wine, scraping the bottom to loosen any brown bits, and bring to a boil. Pour in the chicken broth and balsamic vinegar and bring to a simmer. Cook until the sauce has reduced by a quarter.

5. Return the chicken to the skillet and warm through. Taste and season with additional salt or pepper if needed.

ROAST PRIME RIB

We encourage all vault dwellers to celebrate the holiday season in any way they see fit, but humbly request that a roast be a part of that celebration. This roast is so good, we know that after giving this recipe a try once, you won't need any coercion to make it again.

TEDDY WRIGHT INFORMED ME THAT THE ONLY WAY TO GAIN THE RESPECT OF THE HARBORMEN WAS BY COMPLETING THE "CAPTAIN'S DANCE." IT WAS A ROUGH TRIAL BUT THIS ROAST WAS TOTALLY WORTH IT AND THE PERFECT WAY TO SPICE UP ANY HOLIDAY PARTY!

6 to 8 pounds bone-in prime rib *BRAHMIN RIBS DID THE TRICK HERE.*

2 tablespoons salt

1 tablespoon dried rosemary

8 garlic cloves, finely grated

Pepper

3 celery ribs, cut into large chunks

1 medium fennel bulb, cut into large chunks

1 medium yellow onion, cut into large chunks

3 sprigs fresh rosemary

5 sprigs fresh thyme

FRESH ROSEMARY AND THYME WERE IMPOSSIBLE TO FIND AMONGST THE WASTELAND SCRUB DURING MY ATTEMPT TO MAKE THIS. ASH BLOSSOM SEEMED TO BE A PERFECT WORK-AROUND.

S.P.E.C.I.A.L:
+2 LUCK FOR 4 HOURS

DIFFICULTY:
MEDIUM

PREP TIME:
2 DAYS

COOK TIME:
4 TO 5 HOURS

SERVINGS:
4 TO 8

PAIRS WELL WITH:
INSTAMASH (PAGE 67)

1. Two days before you plan on roasting the prime rib, combine the salt, rosemary, and garlic in a bowl. Rub the mixed seasoning over the entire prime rib. Lay the meat on a baking sheet fitted with a rack and place in the refrigerator uncovered. Allow the prime rib to rest for at least 48 hours and up to 96 hours.

2. Take the prime rib out of the refrigerator for at least one hour before it goes into the oven and allow it to come to room temperature. Adjust an oven rack to the middle-lower position. Preheat the oven to 250°F.

3. Take a deep baking dish with a roasting rack inserted and fill the bottom of the baking dish with celery, fennel, onion, rosemary, and thyme. Heavily season the prime rib with pepper. Lay the prime rib, fat side up, on the roasting rack. Place the meat in the oven and roast until the prime rib reaches the desired internal temperature: 130°F for medium-rare, 3 to 3½ hours; 135°F for medium, 3½ to 4 hours.

4. Remove the prime rib from the oven, loosely cover with aluminum foil, and let rest for 45 minutes. Increase the oven temperature to 500°F. Move the oven rack up to the top-middle of your oven. Remove the aluminum foil from the prime rib and place in the oven. Cook until the fat begins to crisp up, about 8 to 10 minutes. Remove the roast from the oven and place on a cutting board. Remove the bone and slice the meat into ½-to-¾-inch-thick pieces and serve.

SADDLE UP SALISBURY STEAK

Our brilliant scientists successfully reverse-engineered the recipe for Saddle Up Salisbury Steak, provided here for your enjoyment! Our legal team has informed us that the Saddle Up corporation is unlikely to bring this matter up in court in the future as they refused to sign on to our corporate vault partnership program.

S.P.E.C.I.A.L:
+2 INTELLIGENCE FOR
30 MINUTES

DIFFICULTY:
EASY

PREP TIME:
30 MINUTES

COOK TIME:
30 MINUTES

SERVINGS:
5 PATTIES

PAIRS WELL WITH:
BUTTERED NOODLES,
MASHED POTATOES, PEAS,
CORN ON THE COB

PATTIES:

1 pound ground beef

½ teaspoon dried thyme

½ teaspoon black pepper

1 teaspoon salt

¼ teaspoon cayenne pepper

1 teaspoon ground cumin

1 tablespoon ground mustard

1 tablespoon ketchup

1 teaspoon Worcestershire sauce

¼ cup panko bread crumbs

1 egg

1 tablespoon canola oil

GRAVY:

½ tablespoon canola oil

½ medium yellow onion, sliced

1 large king oyster mushroom, sliced

5 shiitake mushrooms, stemmed and sliced

2 cups beef broth, divided

2 teaspoons Dijon mustard

2 teaspoons dried tarragon

2 tablespoons cornstarch

I SUPPOSE A MIX OF BRAIN FUNGUS AND GLOWING FUNGUS WOULD WORK FOR THIS RECIPE.

1. Begin making the patties by using your hands to combine all of the patty ingredients—except the oil—in a large bowl. Split the meat into 5 equal portions and form into patties that are about ¾-inch thick.

2. Heat the canola oil in a large sauté pan or skillet over medium-high heat. Place the patties in the pan and cook until the bottoms have browned, about 2 minutes. Flip and brown the other side, about 2 minutes more. Remove the patties from the pan and set aside. They will still be raw in the middle.

3. To make the gravy, add the ½ tablespoon canola oil to the pan, still over medium-high heat. Add the onion, oyster mushrooms, and shiitake mushrooms, and sauté until softened, about 3 minutes. Add 1½ cups of the beef broth, along with the Dijon mustard and tarragon. Cover and cook for 5 minutes.

4. In a small bowl, stir together the cornstarch and remaining ½ cup beef broth. Slowly add the cornstarch slurry to the pan and whisk together until the gravy thickens slightly.

5. Add the patties back to the pan and reduce the heat to medium. Cover and simmer the patties for 7 minutes. Flip and simmer for another 7 minutes, then serve the patties with noodles or mashed potatoes, topped with the gravy.

SLOW-ROASTED LEG OF ~~LAMB~~ YAO GUAI

Here is a perfect meal for when the family is looking to change things up and get a bit adventurous! That said, please keep your adventure to a minimum as our stock of lamb is a bit scarce. In fact, why not keep things simpler this evening? Perhaps a lovely Salisbury steak (page 109)? You've worked so hard today, why put in the effort? Forget we said anything.

S.P.E.C.I.A.L:
+1 STRENGTH FOR 1 HOUR

5 pounds semi-boneless leg of ~~lamb~~ YAO GUAI

1 garlic bulb, halved

3 medium shallots, quartered

5 sprigs fresh rosemary

5 sprigs fresh mint

Salt and pepper

THE VAULT RAN OUT OF LAMB WELL BEFORE MY TIME, SO I'VE HAD TO IMPROVISE HERE. I TOOK THEIR ADVICE, GOT A BIT ADVENTUROUS, AND MANAGED TO TAKE DOWN A YAO GUAI, SO THAT'LL DO FOR NOW BUT I HAD TO QUADRUPLE THE ROAST TIME. HAVE YOU SEEN HOW HUGE THEIR LEGS ARE?

DIFFICULTY:
MEDIUM

PREP TIME:
2 HOURS

COOK TIME:
3 TO 5 HOURS

SERVINGS:
6 TO 8

PAIRS WELL WITH:
SUGAR-BOMBED CARROTS (PAGE 75)

1. Take the leg of lamb out of the refrigerator at least 1 hour before it goes into the oven so it has time to come to room temperature. Adjust an oven rack to the middle-lower position. Preheat the oven to 300°F. Season the lamb with salt and pepper.

2. Place the lamb, garlic bulb, shallots, rosemary, and mint in a dutch oven or other deep baking tray, and cover. Roast in the oven until the lamb reaches the desired temperature. Use a meat thermometer to confirm the meat's internal temperature: 135°F for medium-rare, 2 to 2½ hours; 140°F for medium, 2½ to 3 hours.

3. Remove from the oven and let rest for 30 minutes. Move the oven rack up so the pot fits in the top half of the oven. Increase the oven temperature to 500°F. Remove the lid and place the pot in the oven. Cook until the fat begins to crisp up, 5 to 10 minutes. Flip the lamb and repeat on the other side, 5 to 10 minutes longer. Let rest for 10 minutes again before carving.

DESSERT

Mutfruit BERRY CRUMBLE

A crumble is one of the best desserts you can have in your repertoire! It provides a wonderful texture and tart taste with half the work of a pie, leaving you more time to enjoy the many amenities of your vault.

PRISCILLA PENSKE OF VAULT 81 HAS DONE SOME AMAZING WORK WITH MUTFRUIT AS SHE CONTINUES TO SCIENTIFICALLY IMPROVE THE FLAVOR AND TEXTURE. WITH A BIT OF EXPERIMENTING, I WAS ABLE TO RE-CREATE THIS CRUMBLE USING HER FRUIT. I JUST HAD TO TRADE HER FOR A BAG OF FERTILIZER.

S.P.E.C.I.A.L:
+2 AGILITY FOR 2 HOURS

DIFFICULTY:
EASY

PREP TIME:
30 MINUTES

COOK TIME:
30 MINUTES

SERVINGS:
6

PAIRS WELL WITH:
VANILLA ICE CREAM

FILLING:

2 cups blueberries

2 cups blackberries

1 tablespoon lemon zest

2 tablespoons lemon juice

½ cup granulated sugar

½ cup honey

1 teaspoon ground nutmeg

1 teaspoon salt

2 tablespoons cornstarch

USE AN EQUAL AMOUNT OF MUTFRUIT TO REPLACE THESE INGREDIENTS.

TOPPING:

¼ cup all-purpose flour

½ cup rolled oats

¼ cup brown sugar

½ teaspoon ground cloves

1 teaspoon ground coriander

1 teaspoon ground cinnamon

½ teaspoon salt

5 tablespoons cold unsalted butter, cubed

1. To make the filling: Preheat the oven to 375°F. Combine the filling ingredients in a medium bowl and mix well. Spoon the filling into two 5-inch ramekins.

2. To make the topping: Combine the flour, oats, brown sugar, cloves, coriander, and salt in another medium bowl. Add the cubed butter. Using your hands, combine the butter with the dry ingredients until it resembles coarse meal.

3. Cover each of the ramekins with the crumble topping. Bake for 45 to 55 minutes, until the crumble is golden brown.

DANDY BOY APPLES

Advances in candy science have resulted in a wide variety of preserved fruits for you to enjoy while you reside in our vaults. We have yet to preserve the integrity of our test subjects' teeth, but this was already covered in their trial waivers.

THE BOX WAS RIGHT—THESE THINGS NEVER GO BAD. I KEEP FINDING BOXES OF DANDY BOY APPLES THAT STILL TASTE FRESH. WHATEVER THEY'RE USING IN THE COATING MUST BE PRESERVING THE APPLES.

4 Fuji apples

¾ cup water

½ cup light corn syrup

2 cups sugar

½ teaspoon rosemary extract (optional)

8 drops red food coloring

I WISH I HAD A BETTER REPLACEMENT FOR APPLES. CRUNCHY MUTFRUIT IS CLOSE BUT THEY'RE STILL SO MEALY.

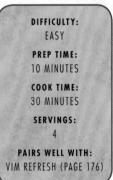

S.P.E.C.I.A.L:
+2 ENDURANCE
FOR 1 HOUR

DIFFICULTY:
EASY

PREP TIME:
10 MINUTES

COOK TIME:
30 MINUTES

SERVINGS:
4

PAIRS WELL WITH:
VIM REFRESH (PAGE 176)

1. Line a baking sheet with parchment paper and set aside. Prepare the apples by inserting a skewer through the top of each apple. Firmly push the skewer in until it is about halfway through the apple.

2. Combine the water, corn syrup, and sugar in a deep saucepan over high heat. Using a candy thermometer, boil the candy mixture until it reaches 300°F, then remove the saucepan from the heat. Stir in the rosemary extract, if using, and red food coloring. Tilt the pot to the side and roll the apples in the candy mixture until fully coated. Place the apples on the prepared baking sheet to cool and harden.

MULLED PEARS

Why drink wine to celebrate the end of a meal when you can eat your wine instead? That is the question we posed to our scientists and what led them to this delicious creation!

S.P.E.C.I.A.L:
+1 INTELLIGENCE FOR
2 HOURS

DIFFICULTY:
EASY

PREP TIME:
10 MINUTES

COOK TIME:
30 MINUTES

SERVINGS:
5

PAIRS WELL WITH:
WHIPPED CREAM
OR ICE CREAM

1 cinnamon stick

3 cardamom pods

10 cloves

3 star anise

1 orange, sliced

1 lime, sliced

One 750-ml bottle red wine

1½ cups pomegranate juice

¾ cup brown sugar

5 pears, peeled

1. Combine everything but the pears in a large pot over medium heat. Bring to a boil then reduce heat to medium-low. Add the peeled pears and simmer for 15 to 20 minutes, until the pears are soft all the way through but not yet mushy.

2. Remove the pears and place on a plate. Increase the heat to medium-high and heat until the liquid reduces to a syrup. Strain the syrup through a mesh strainer to remove all the spices and fruit. Serve the poached pears covered in syrup.

I THINK I'VE FOUND EXACTLY
ONE FRESH PEAR IN MY TRAVELS
AROUND THE WASTELAND, BUT
I THINK IT WOULD BE WORTH IT
TO USE THE NEXT ONE I FIND IN
THIS RECIPE.

TAPIOCA PUDDING

Please follow Vault-Tec™ scheduling and only use the mess hall food reconstitution system to output tapioca pudding at the designated time: Monday evenings. It is crucial to perform the proper maintenance necessary to prevent any strange discoloration.

Even when we followed the maintenance instructions, our machine started churning out orange-colored pudding. I may experiment with turning up the mango flavor and hope no one notices.

S.P.E.C.I.A.L:
+1 LUCK
FOR 30 MINUTES

DIFFICULTY:
EASY

PREP TIME:
12 HOURS

COOK TIME:
30 MINUTES

SERVINGS:
4

PAIRS WELL WITH:
FRESH MANGO AND
COCONUT CHIPS

⅓ cup small pearl tapioca

3½ cups coconut milk, divided

2 egg yolks

¼ cup cornstarch

1 large mango, diced

Juice of ½ lime

¼ cup sugar

1 teaspoon salt

1 teaspoon vanilla extract

Few drops of orange food dye (optional)

1. Place the pearl tapioca and 1¾ cups of the coconut milk in a medium saucepan and allow the tapioca to soak for 30 minutes.

2. In a medium bowl, beat the egg yolks and cornstarch together.

3. Using a blender, puree the remaining 1¾ cups coconut milk, mango, and lime juice together. Add half the coconut and mango puree to the bowl with the beaten egg yolks, then whisk together.

4. Place the saucepan with the tapioca and coconut milk over medium heat and add the sugar and salt. Bring to a simmer, stirring constantly. Reduce the heat to low and continue to cook and stir for 10 minutes, until the tapioca becomes clear.

5. Transfer ¼ cup of the hot coconut milk mixture into the beaten egg yolks and whisk together. Repeat this process six more times, then pour the contents of the bowl back into the saucepan and whisk until it thickens.

6. Remove from the heat and stir in the vanilla extract. Mix the remaining pureed mango into the saucepan and add the orange food dye, if using. Split the pudding into 4 cups. Cover and refrigerate overnight to set.

FRUIT CREAM PIE

If you're lucky enough to reside in a vault, you'll enjoy cutting-edge botany techniques that will provide you with fresh fruit for pies for years to come!

I COULDN'T FIND ANY ENTRIES ON BANANAS IN THE VAULT MANIFESTS, BUT A DOCTOR I CAME ACROSS HAD A PATIENT WHO WAS CONVINCED BANANAS WERE REAL AND THOUGHT THAT BANANAS COULD FLY. AND, APPARENTLY, PERSUADE OTHERS THAT THEY CAN TALK. STRANGE.

S.P.E.C.I.A.L:
+1 CHARISMA
FOR 1 HOUR

DIFFICULTY:
MEDIUM

PREP TIME:
5 HOURS

COOK TIME:
1 HOUR

SERVINGS:
8 SLICES

PAIRS WELL WITH:
DADDY-O (PAGE 183)

CRUST:

2 cups all-purpose flour

1 teaspoon ground nutmeg

2 teaspoons ground ginger

½ teaspoon salt

1 teaspoon sugar

12 tablespoons (1½ sticks) cold unsalted butter, cubed

¼ cup cold water

FILLING:

1 cup sugar, divided

5 tablespoons cornstarch

5 egg yolks

2½ cups coconut milk

½ vanilla bean, split and scraped

1 teaspoon salt

2 tablespoons unsalted butter

2 teaspoons vanilla extract

3 bananas, sliced

½ cup sliced jackfruit (optional)

WHIPPED CREAM:

1½ cups cold heavy cream

2 teaspoons vanilla extract

2 tablespoons sugar

TO MAKE THE CRUST:

1. Preheat the oven to 375°F. Combine the flour, nutmeg, ginger, salt, and sugar in a food processor. Add the cubed butter and pulse until it resembles coarse meal. Slowly add the cold water and mix until a dough forms.

2. Knead the dough on the countertop for 5 minutes. Form a ball, wrap in plastic wrap, and allow the dough to rest in the refrigerator for at least 10 minutes.

3. Roll out the dough to ⅛-to-¼ inch thickness and place in a 9½-inch pie dish. Leave any extra dough to hang slightly over the sides. Place parchment paper over the pie crust. Fill with pie weights, rice, or dry beans to keep the base of the pie from rising while it cooks. Bake for 20 minutes. Remove the parchment paper and rice or beans. If the crust has not browned completely, place back in the oven and bake until golden brown. Set on a cooling rack and allow to completely cool.

Continued on next page

TO MAKE THE FILLING:

4. Combine ½ cup of the sugar, cornstarch, and egg yolks in a medium bowl and set aside. In a deep saucepan over medium-high heat, add the coconut milk, vanilla bean (scraped seeds and full bean), the remaining ½ cup sugar, and salt. Bring to a simmer and reduce heat to medium, whisking constantly.

5. Scoop ½ cup of the heated mixture and add into the bowl with the egg yolks and whisk until well combined. Add another ½ cup of the hot mixture and whisk thoroughly again. Slowly whisk the egg yolk mixture into the saucepan and increase the heat to medium-high. Whisk until it thickens. Remove from the heat and add the butter and vanilla.

6. Pour half of the pudding filling into the pie crust. Add the bananas and jackfruit. Add the remaining filling on top. Cover with plastic wrap and refrigerate for at least 3 hours.

TO MAKE THE WHIPPED CREAM:

7. Place the heavy cream, vanilla extract, and sugar into the bowl of a stand mixer fitted with the whisk attachment. Mix until the whipped cream forms stiff peaks. Top the pie with the whipped cream and serve.

PERFECTLY PRESERVED PIE

After retrieving a delicious slice of perfectly preserved pie from the Port-A-Diner,
Vault-Tec™ whisked it away to the lab and came up with this real humdinger of a dessert.

*WHILE THIS IS A SATISFYING DESSERT TO MAKE, IT MAKES
ME APPRECIATE HOW CONVENIENT IT IS TO JUST PICK UP A
200-YEAR-OLD SLICE FROM JUST ABOUT ANY PORT-A-DINER.*

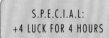

S.P.E.C.I.A.L:
+4 LUCK FOR 4 HOURS

DIFFICULTY:
HARD

PREP TIME:
2 HOURS

COOK TIME:
3 HOURS

SERVINGS:
8 SLICES

PAIRS WELL WITH:
RED WINE

CHEESECAKE:

¼ cup heavy cream

½ vanilla bean, split and scraped

1 pound cream cheese, at room temperature

¾ cup sugar

3 eggs

½ cup sour cream

Pinch of salt

2 tablespoons cornstarch

1 tablespoon vanilla extract

TOPPING:

2 pounds strawberries, hulled

1 cinnamon stick

¾ cup sugar

1 tablespoon vanilla extract

Pinch of salt

2 tablespoons cornstarch

3 tablespoons water

3 cups Caramel Buttercream Frosting (page 15)

TO MAKE THE CHEESECAKE:

1. Preheat the oven to 275°F. Combine the heavy cream and the scraped vanilla bean in a small bowl and set aside.

2. In a bowl of a stand mixer fitted with the whisk attachment, whip the cream cheese until smooth. You will need to scrape down the sides a few times to make sure all of the cream cheese is completely smooth. Add the sugar and mix well. Next, add the eggs one at a time.

3. Remove the vanilla bean from the heavy cream. Pour the heavy cream, sour cream, salt, cornstarch, and vanilla extract into the cream cheese mixture. Mix well and scrape the sides to incorporate everything completely.

4. Wrap the outside of a 9-inch springform pan in aluminum foil. This will prevent any water from entering the pan. Butter the inside of the pan. Carefully line the pan with parchment paper. All of these steps will prevent the cheesecake from sticking, making it easier to remove from the pan.

Continued on next page

5. Pour the batter into the pan and rap the pan against the counter several times to remove air bubbles. Place the cake pan in a large, deep baking tray. Pour hot water in the baking tray until it is about halfway up on the cake pan. This is done to avoid harshly cooking the cake and to prevent cracks from forming on the top. Bake for 1 hour, until set.

6. Turn off the heat and keep the cheesecake in the oven for another hour. This allows the cheesecake to finish cooking inside without cracking the top. Remove from the oven and the deep baking pan and cool to room temperature, then refrigerate for at least 4 hours (overnight is best).

TO MAKE THE TOPPING:

7. Place the strawberries in a blender and puree until smooth. Pour the pureed strawberries through a mesh strainer to remove the seeds. Place into a large saucepan with the cinnamon stick over medium-high heat. Bring to a boil, then reduce the heat to low and add the sugar, vanilla extract, and salt. Simmer for 10 minutes.

8. In a small bowl, combine the cornstarch and water. Remove the cinnamon stick and add the cornstarch slurry to the saucepan and whisk until it has slightly thickened. Allow to cool and then cover and place in the refrigerator. The sauce will fully thicken as it cools, so allow it to refrigerate for at least 2 hours (overnight is best).

FOR ASSEMBLY:

9. Slice a piece of the cheesecake and drizzle with the strawberry sauce. Place the caramel buttercream into a pastry bag with a closed star tip. Place a small dollop of caramel buttercream on top of the sliced cheesecake.

BIRTHDAY CAKE

A good birthday cake recipe is a requirement for any vault dweller!
Mandatory birthday party decorations including "Happy Birthday" signage,
balloons, and party hats can be found in every vault.

S.P.E.C.I.A.L:
+1 LUCK FOR 1 YEAR

DIFFICULTY:
HARD

PREP TIME:
30 MINUTES

COOK TIME:
45 MINUTES

SERVINGS:
8 SLICES

PAIRS WELL WITH:
BIRTHDAY HATS,
NUKA-COLA (PAGE 165)

CAKE:

3 cups cake flour

1 tablespoon baking powder

1 teaspoon salt

2 teaspoons ground cardamom

1 teaspoon ground ginger

½ teaspoon ground cinnamon

1 cup (2 sticks) unsalted butter, at room
   temperature

1¾ cups sugar

2 whole eggs

2 egg whites

3 tablespoons vanilla extract

1 cup whole milk

½ cup Greek yogurt

FROSTING:

2 cups mascarpone cheese

1 vanilla bean, seeds scraped and pod
   discarded

2 teaspoons vanilla extract

¾ cup half-and-half

¾ cup heavy cream

½ teaspoon salt

3 cups confectioners' sugar

*BIRTHDAYS IN THE VAULT
WERE . . . INTERESTING.
THE MOST MEMORABLE
PART WAS ALWAYS WHEN
OUR MISTER HANDY
"SERVED" THE CAKE.*

TO MAKE THE CAKE:

1. Preheat the oven to 350°F. Spray two 8-inch cake pans with nonstick spray. Combine the
    cake flour, baking powder, salt, cardamom, ginger, and cinnamon in a medium bowl and
    set aside. In a large bowl, combine the butter and sugar and mix until smooth. Mix in the
    eggs, egg whites, and vanilla.

2. Add half of the dry ingredients into the large bowl and mix well. Add the milk and mix.
    Add the remaining dry ingredients and the Greek yogurt, and mix until completely
    smooth. Divide the batter evenly between the two prepared pans. Bake for 35 to 40
    minutes, until a toothpick inserted into the center of a cake comes out clean.

Continued on next page

TO MAKE THE FROSTING:

3. In the bowl of a stand mixer, combine the mascarpone cheese and seeds from the vanilla bean and mix together on medium until well mixed. While the mixer is running, add the vanilla extract, half-and-half, and heavy cream. Then gradually add the confectioners' sugar and whip until stiff peaks form, about 5 minutes.

TO ASSEMBLE:

4. Once the cake layers have fully cooled, level both layers by slicing off the rounded top of the cake with a serrated knife. Place one of the layers on a serving plate.

5. Using a spatula, add a generous portion of frosting on top, about ½ inch in thickness, and spread evenly. Carefully place the second cake layer on top of the frosting. Then, frost the entire exterior of the cake with the remaining frosting. Refrigerate for at least 10 minutes or until just before you are going to serve. Top with birthday candles and serve.

OLD LADY PALMER'S SWEETROLL

This delicious sticky sweetroll is the perfect dessert to celebrate any occasion!
Is it your birthday? An anniversary? The world ended and you had to flee
to a Vault-Tec™ vault? You got a promotion at the Nuka-Cola plant in your vault?
All great reasons to make this and enjoy!

SWEETROLLS:

1 cup lukewarm (110°F) milk

2¼ teaspoons active dry yeast

½ cup (1 stick) unsalted butter, divided

¼ cup granulated sugar

1 teaspoon kosher salt

1 large egg

1 teaspoon vanilla extract

¾ teaspoon ground star anise, divided

3½ cups all-purpose flour

⅓ cup brown sugar

1½ tablespoons ground cinnamon

¼ teaspoon ground star anise

½ teaspoon ground cardamom

ICING:

4 ounces cream cheese, at room temperature

1½ cups confectioners' sugar

Pinch of ground cinnamon

½ teaspoon salt

½ teaspoon vanilla extract

5 tablespoons unsalted butter, melted

2 tablespoons milk

1. Begin making the sweetroll dough by combining the lukewarm milk and yeast in a small cup.

2. In a stand mixer fitted with the dough attachment, combine 4 tablespoons of the butter, sugar, and salt. Once well combined, add the egg and vanilla. Then pour in the milk and yeast mixture. Next, add ¼ teaspoon of the star anise and the flour. Mix until combined, but do not overmix, or the dough will be tough.

3. After the flour has incorporated, take the dough out of the bowl and knead by hand for 5 minutes. Place the dough in a greased bowl (use nonstick spray) and cover. Allow to rise for at least 2 hours, until doubled in size.

Continued on next page

4. After the dough has risen, preheat the oven to 350°F and grease two round cake pans (use nonstick spray).

5. In a small bowl, combine the brown sugar, cinnamon, star anise, and cardamom.

6. Roll the dough out into a rectangular shape without rolling it too thin. Take the remaining butter, soften it, then spread it over the top of the dough using your hands. Sprinkle the cinnamon mixture over the buttered dough.

7. Tightly roll the dough lengthwise. Use a serrated knife to cut 1½-inch pieces. You should end up with 12 to 14 pieces. Place 6 to 7 of the buns in the two prepared pans about ½ inch apart. Cover the cake pan with a towel and allow the buns to rise for another 15 to 30 minutes. Remove the towel and bake the buns for 25 minutes, until golden brown.

8. While the buns are baking, make the icing by thoroughly mixing the cream cheese, confectioners' sugar, cinnamon, and salt together in a medium bowl. Pour the melted butter in the bowl and mix. Add the milk and mix until smooth.

9. When you take the buns out of the oven, immediately drizzle the icing on top and serve.

I'VE ALWAYS WONDERED WHAT I WOULD DO IF SOMEONE THREATENED TO TAKE MY SWEETROLL FROM ME. PERHAPS I'D JUST EAT IT IN A RUSH OR MAYBE JUST THROW IT ON THE GROUND AND ESCAPE IN THE CONFUSION.

FANCY LADS SNACK CAKES

We know all vault dwellers love that classic Fancy Lads Snack Cakes jingle you hear on the radio. You get a big delight in every bite, they're so tasty and so sweet! We've packed our vaults with boxes of them. Though if you're feeling a hankering to tinker in your fully stocked vault kitchen, we've convinced Fancy Lads to give us their secret recipe for your favorite cakes, found exclusively in this cookbook!

CAKE:

1 cup (2 sticks) unsalted butter,
   at room temperature

1¾ cups sugar

4 eggs, at room temperature

2 tablespoons vanilla extract

3½ cups cake flour

¼ teaspoon ground allspice

2 teaspoons baking powder

1 teaspoon salt

1 cup milk

½ cup Greek yogurt

MARSHMALLOW FILLING:

½ cup (1 stick) unsalted butter

¼ cup cream cheese

¾ cup marshmallow cream

1 tablespoon vanilla extract

2 cups confectioners' sugar

2 tablespoons heavy cream

WHITE FROSTING:

24 ounces white vanilla candy melts

4 tablespoons shortening

TO MAKE THE CAKE:

1. Preheat the oven to 350°F and grease a 10-by-15-inch baking pan well with butter. In a large bowl, cream the butter and sugar together. Add the eggs and vanilla, then mix well.

2. In a medium bowl, combine the cake flour, allspice, baking powder, and salt. Add half of the flour mixture to the wet ingredients and stir. Add the milk and the remaining flour mixture and stir to combine. Finally, add the Greek yogurt and mix well.

3. Pour the batter into the prepared baking pan. Bake for 30 to 40 minutes, until a toothpick inserted in the center comes out clean. Transfer to wire rack and allow the cake to completely cool, then refrigerate for at least 30 minutes.

Continued on next page

TO MAKE THE MARSHMALLOW FILLING:

4. Combine the butter, cream cheese, and marshmallow cream in the bowl of a stand mixer fitted with the whisk attachment. Add the vanilla and beat until smooth. Add the confectioners' sugar and heavy cream and mix until well combined. Refrigerate for at least 30 minutes.

TO ASSEMBLE THE CAKE:

5. Remove the cake from the refrigerator and cut it into an even number of equal-sized rectangles.

6. Place the marshmallow filling into a piping bag fitted with a large round tip. Carefully layer half of the cakes with the marshmallow filling, then top with a plain cake. Refrigerate again for at least 2 hours.

7. Make the white frosting when the cakes have finished chilling. Combine the candy melts and shortening in a large bowl and heat in a microwave to melt. Do this in 30-second intervals and mix in between each heating. Repeat until smooth.

8. Place a wire rack on top of a baking sheet and spray with nonstick spray. Once the white frosting is melted, take the cakes and dip each of the four sides in the frosting so every side (except the top and bottom) is completely covered, then place the cake on the wire rack. Repeat until all cakes are covered.

9. Allow the sides of the cake to harden a bit. Once hardened (you might have to reheat the white frosting) dip the tops of the cakes. Allow the tops to harden as well, then serve.

SLOCUM'S BUZZBITES

We have quite a special treat for you today: the fabled recipe for Slocum's Buzzbites! The actual product was never sold due to some minor third-degree burns, but we absolutely love these tasty bites!

Are they seriously suggesting injecting boiling hot coffee? Why don't I replace that with something a little less hazardous and a lot more sweet?

S.P.E.C.I.A.L.:
+3 AGILITY FOR 3 HOURS

DIFFICULTY:
HARD

PREP TIME:
1 HOUR

COOK TIME:
30 MINUTES

SERVINGS:
40 TO 60

PAIRS WELL WITH:
HOT COFFEE

DOUGHNUT DOUGH:

1 cup milk

2 tablespoons unsalted butter

1 cinnamon stick

2 star anise

2 cardamom pods

3 whole cloves

3 teaspoons active dry yeast

3¼ cups bread flour

¼ cup sugar

½ teaspoon salt

2 eggs

1 teaspoon vanilla extract

Peanut oil for frying

COFFEE FILLING:

4 egg yolks

½ cup heavy cream

⅓ cup cornstarch

½ cup prepared coffee

1 cup milk

¾ cup sugar

1 teaspoon salt

1 tablespoon ground cinnamon

1 teaspoon ground ginger

1 teaspoon ground cardamom

¼ teaspoon pepper

1½ tablespoons unsalted butter

TOPPING:

1 cup sugar

1 tablespoon ground cinnamon

TO MAKE THE DOUGHNUT DOUGH:

1. Place the milk, butter, cinnamon, star anise, cardamom, and cloves in a medium saucepan over medium heat. Bring to a boil, then reduce the heat to low and allow to simmer for 5 minutes. Take off the heat and, using a thermometer, allow the mixture to cool to 100°F to 110°F. Remove the spices and stir in the yeast. Let rest for 5 minutes until the yeast begins to froth up.

2. In the bowl of a stand mixer fitted with a dough hook attachment, combine the milk mixture with the flour, sugar, and salt and mix until lightly incorporated. Add the eggs and vanilla extract, and mix on medium speed until the dough is smooth, 5 to 10 minutes. After the dough has come together, place in a lightly oiled bowl and cover. Allow the dough to rise for at least 2 hours, until it has doubled in size.

Continued on next page

TO MAKE THE COFFEE FILLING:

3. Make the filling while the dough is rising. Combine the egg yolks, heavy cream, and cornstarch in a medium bowl. Whisk together the coffee, milk, sugar, salt, cinnamon, ginger, cardamom, and pepper in a saucepan over medium-high heat and bring to a boil. Reduce the heat to low.

4. Slowly add ½ cup of the heated mixture into the bowl with the egg yolks and heavy cream while whisking continuously to avoid scrambling the egg yolks. Add another ½ cup of the hot mixture while whisking, and continue until you've added about three-quarters of the hot mixture into the bowl. Then transfer the mixture back to the saucepan.

5. Increase the heat to medium and whisk the mixture constantly until the filling thickens. Once thickened, remove from the heat and whisk in the butter. Transfer to a container and wrap the top with plastic wrap to cool. Refrigerate until you are ready to fill the doughnuts.

TO MAKE THE DOUGHNUTS:

6. Remove the dough from its bowl and place onto a lightly floured surface. Punch the dough down and roll out to a half-inch thickness. Cut out the dough with a 2-inch round cutter and place the rounds on parchment paper. Cover with plastic wrap and set aside for at least 30 minutes, allowing the dough to rise again.

7. Fill a deep pot with 2 inches of peanut oil and heat over medium heat to 350°F. Line a plate with paper towels. Place 5 to 8 doughnuts in the oil and cook for 1 minute, flip them, then cook for 1 minute more. Remove the doughnuts from the oil and place them onto the paper towel–lined plate. Repeat with the remaining doughnuts. The oil temperature might drop between each batch, so be sure to let the oil heat back up to 350°F before adding each set of doughnuts.

8. After all the doughnuts have cooled, fill a pastry bag fitted with a round tip with the coffee filling. Take a chopstick and poke a hole into a doughnut. Insert the tip of the pastry bag into the doughnut and squeeze the bag gently to fill the doughnut. Repeat with all the doughnuts.

9. Combine the sugar and cinnamon on a plate or in a shallow bowl. Toss the doughnuts in the sugar and cinnamon mixture and serve.

SPICY CHOCOLATE BUNDT CAKE

Keep an eye on those calendars for the Annual Vault Bake-Off! This year Bundt cakes are the only accepted cake. Please also note that every vault dweller has received the same mandatory reading and thus is in possession of the same recipe, so make yours something S.P.E.C.I.A.L.

S.P.E.C.I.A.L:
+1 INTELLIGENCE
FOR 2 HOURS

DIFFICULTY:
MEDIUM

PREP TIME:
30 MINUTES

COOK TIME:
1 HOUR

SERVINGS:
8 TO 16 SLICES

PAIRS WELL WITH:
A COLD GLASS OF MILK

CAKE:

⅔ cup cocoa powder

2 cups all-purpose flour

1 teaspoon baking soda

1 teaspoon baking powder

½ teaspoon salt

½ cup unsalted butter, at room temperature

1 cup sour cream

1½ cups sugar

2 TEASPOONS GROUND CINNAMON

1 TEASPOON CAYENNE PEPPER

2 eggs

2 teaspoons vanilla extract

1⅔ cups buttermilk

GLAZE:

2 tablespoons unsalted butter

¼ cup heavy cream

½ cup confectioners' sugar

½ cup dark chocolate chips

1 teaspoon vanilla extract

I FOUND A CASE OF CINNAMON AND CAYENNE PEPPER IN THE VAULT STORAGE. SEEMS SOMEONE STORED IT PRETTY FAR IN THE BACK. THIS IS MY SECRET ADDITION TO THE NORMAL CHOCOLATE BUNDT CAKE EVERYONE MAKES, SO YOU CAN CONSIDER THIS OPTIONAL, BUT I WAS THE CHAMP THREE YEARS IN A ROW!

TO MAKE THE CAKE:

1. Preheat the oven to 350°F. Spray a Bundt cake pan with nonstick spray. Combine the cocoa powder, flour, baking soda, baking powder, cinnamon, cayenne pepper, and salt in a medium bowl and set aside.

2. Combine the butter, sour cream, and sugar in a large bowl and mix until smooth. Add the eggs and vanilla, and mix to combine.

3. Add half of the dry ingredients to the bowl with the wet ingredients and mix well. Then add the buttermilk and continue to mix. Add the remaining dry ingredients and mix until completely smooth.

4. Pour the batter into the prepared pan. Bake for 45 to 55 minutes or until a toothpick inserted into the cake comes out clean. Allow to completely cool on a rack before glazing.

TO MAKE THE GLAZE:

5. Melt the butter in a medium saucepan over medium-high heat then add the heavy cream and confectioners' sugar and whisk to combine. Add the chocolate and vanilla extract, then whisk continuously until the chocolate has melted completely.

6. Turn off the heat. Cool for 5 minutes before pouring over the cake.

CHOCOLATE CHIP COOKIES

Chocolate chip cookies: the great American classic. No recipe book would be complete without them, and as they're not addictive, feel free to eat as many as you'd like while relaxing in your vault!

1 cup (2 sticks) unsalted butter, at room temperature

¾ cup granulated sugar

¼ cup brown sugar

1 egg, at room temperature

1 teaspoon vanilla extract

1 teaspoon almond extract

2 cups all-purpose flour

½ cup cocoa powder

1 teaspoon baking soda

1 teaspoon salt

1 cup white chocolate chips

¾ cup dried cranberries (optional)

Rose's Bed and Breakfast was a welcome respite after a long trek through the wastelands of Northern California. You get a free cookie from Rose when you order a glass of water. It's truly the perfect way to end a long adventure.

As with Piper's Special Soda Bread (page 77), you can leave some mutfruit out in the sun to dry as a cranberry alternative.

1. In a large bowl, cream the butter, granulated sugar, and brown sugar together. Add the egg and both the vanilla and almond extracts. Scrape the sides and bottom of the bowl as needed to fully incorporate the wet ingredients.

2. In a small bowl, combine the flour, cocoa powder, baking soda, and salt. Slowly add the flour mixture to the wet ingredients until well combined. Fold in the white chocolate chips and dried cranberries, if using. Cover the bowl with plastic wrap and refrigerate overnight, or up to 2 days.

3. Preheat the oven to 350°F. Line two baking sheets with parchment paper. Drop the dough onto the cookie sheet in heaping tablespoons, roughly 2 inches apart. Bake for 10 to 15 minutes, until the edges crisp up, rotating the pan once during baking. Allow to cool completely on a rack.

MUSHROOM CLOUDS

Here at Vault-Tec™, we like to celebrate the wonderful powers of atomic energy.
All of our modern comforts stem from this wonderful technology! These mushroom cloud
meringues are the perfect bit of corporate fun and a favorite at company functions.

S.P.E.C.I.A.L:
+1 ENDURANCE
FOR 30 MINUTES

DIFFICULTY:
HARD

PREP TIME:
12 HOURS

COOK TIME:
2 HOURS

SERVINGS:
40 TO 50

PAIRS WELL WITH:
NUKA-COLA QUANTUM
(PAGE 166)

1¼ cups sugar

5 egg whites, at room temperature

¼ teaspoon cream of tartar

¼ cup dark chocolate chips

¼ cup dark chocolate cocoa powder

1. Preheat the oven to 200°F. Pour the sugar into a blender or food processor fitted with a metal blade. Cover the machine with a towel to reduce the amount of escaped sugar dust. Blend for 1 minute to make superfine sugar.

2. Place the egg whites and cream of tartar in a bowl of a stand mixer fitted with the whisk attachment. Whisk at medium speed until the eggs form soft peaks. Increase the speed to high and continue beating the eggs while slowly adding the superfine sugar. Blend until the meringues form stiff peaks and the egg whites are glossy.

3. Spoon the egg whites into a piping bag fitted with a round tip. Place a piece of parchment paper on a baking tray. To create the mushroom caps, hold the bag perpendicular to the parchment paper and squeeze out round discs of meringue about 1½ inches wide. To create the stems, squeeze some meringue onto the sheet, then pull the bag up to create a cone shape just under 1½ inches tall. Be sure to create an equal number of caps and stems.

4. Bake the cookies for 90 minutes. Turn off the heat and open the oven door slightly and let the meringues sit overnight to complete the drying process.

5. To construct the mushroom clouds, melt the chocolate chips. Spread a small amount on the bottom of a mushroom cap then gently press the cap on the top of a stem and let the chocolate dry. Once dried, carefully brush the bottom of the stem with cocoa powder to give the mushroom an extra-explosive look.

Buffout MATCHA COOKIES

S.P.E.C.I.A.L:
+2 STRENGTH AND ENDURANCE FOR 1 HOUR

DIFFICULTY:
EASY

PREP TIME:
1 HOUR

COOK TIME:
20 MINUTES

SERVINGS:
36 COOKIES

PAIRS WELL WITH:
HOT TEA

1 cup (2 sticks) unsalted butter, softened

½ cup confectioners' sugar

2 teaspoons vanilla extract

½ teaspoon almond extract

1½ cups all-purpose flour

½ cup almond flour

1 tablespoon matcha powder

1 teaspoon salt

¼ teaspoon ground nutmeg

1. In a medium bowl, combine the butter and confectioners' sugar. Add the vanilla and almond extracts. Stir in the remaining ingredients. Cover a baking sheet with parchment paper and flour. Do not use nonstick spray as this will cause the cookies to flatten as they cook.

2. Take a tablespoon of the cookie dough and roll it into a ball in your hands. Gently press the ball down onto the parchment paper to form a large disk. With a knife, cut a cross over the cookie. Repeat with the remaining dough. Place the tray in the refrigerator for 1 hour.

3. Preheat the oven to 325°F. Bake the cookies for 15 to 20 minutes, until set or until crispy. Allow the cookies to completely cool.

RADIOACTIVE GUMDROPS

Radioactive gumdrops are one of our favorite candies! If we don't have a chance to run to the nearby Super-Duper Mart to grab a few, we'll throw together a batch in the lab.

GUMDROPS:

3 tablespoons unflavored gelatin

1¾ cups cold water, divided

1 teaspoon lemon extract

1 teaspoon orange extract

½ teaspoon rosemary extract (optional)

10 drops green food coloring

2 cups sugar

¼ cup lime juice

2 teaspoons lime zest

2 teaspoons citric acid

COATING:

¼ cup sugar

1 tablespoon citric acid (less if you want these to be less tart)

1. In a large heat-resistant bowl, combine the gelatin and ¾ cup of the water. Set aside.

2. In a small bowl, combine the lemon extract, orange extract, rosemary extract (if using), and food coloring. Set aside.

3. Combine the remaining 1 cup water and the sugar in a medium saucepan over medium-high heat. Bring to a slight boil and simmer for 5 minutes on medium-low, then pour the hot sugar water into the large gelatin mixture bowl. Stir until the gelatin is completely dissolved.

4. Add extracts, lime juice, lime zest, and citric acid to the gelatin bowl and stir until incorporated. Prepare a 10-by-10-inch pan by lining it with aluminum foil and spraying with nonstick spray. Pour the mixture into the prepared pan. Cover and refrigerate for at least 8 hours.

Continued on next page

5. Line a large baking sheet with parchment paper and set a wire rack on top. Remove the cooled candy by pulling the aluminum from the pan. Flip the candy onto a cutting board and remove the aluminum foil. Cut the candy into bite-size square pieces and place on the wire rack. Leave the candy sitting out at room temperature for 10 hours.

6. To make the coating, combine the sugar and citric acid on a plate. Roll the gumdrops in the sugar mixture. Place the coated pieces back on the wire rack, making sure they are not touching. Refrigerate, uncovered, for another 10 hours to dry out. After this last drying stage, they are ready to eat. These are best served cold and will stay fresh in the refrigerator for up to 2 weeks.

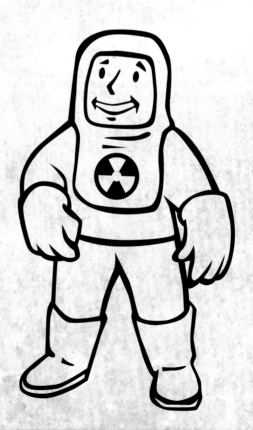

MISSISSIPPI QUANTUM PIE

NUKA-COLA QUANTUM'S BLUE COLOR IS SO AMAZING.

CRUST:

20 ounces (450 grams) chocolate crème
    sandwich cookies

⅔ cup walnuts

5 tablespoons unsalted butter, melted

¾ cup cocoa powder

¾ teaspoon salt

¾ cup dark chocolate chips

4 tablespoons (½ stick) unsalted butter

1¾ teaspoons vanilla extract

CHOCOLATE PUDDING:

⅔ cup heavy cream

5 egg yolks

1 cup granulated sugar, divided

⅓ cup cornstarch

2½ cups milk

QUANTUM WHIPPED CREAM:

1½ cups heavy whipping cream

½ teaspoon lemon extract

½ teaspoon orange extract

20 drops neon blue food dye

3 tablespoons confectioners' sugar

TO MAKE THE CRUST:

1. Preheat the oven to 375°F. Spray a 9-inch springform pan with nonstick spray and line bottom and sides with parchment paper.

2. Place the chocolate crème sandwich cookies and walnuts into a food processor and pulse to a fine crumble. Add the butter and pulse again until the butter is incorporated throughout the crumbs.

3. Pour the mixture into the prepared springform pan and, using your fingers, press the crumbs into a thin layer across the bottom with a 2½-inch-tall crust up the sides. Bake for 10 minutes. Set aside to cool.

Continued on next page

TO MAKE THE PUDDING:

4. In a medium bowl, combine the heavy cream, egg yolks, ¼ cup of the granulated sugar, and cornstarch and set aside. In a medium saucepan, whisk together the milk, the remaining ¾ cup sugar, cocoa powder, and salt over medium-high heat. Once the cocoa powder has dissolved, add the dark chocolate chips. Heat the mixture up until right before it would boil, whisking as it heats to avoid it sticking to the pan.

5. Scoop ½ cup of the heated mixture into the bowl with the egg yolks and whisk until well combined. Add another ½ cup of the hot mixture and whisk thoroughly again. Slowly whisk the egg yolk mixture into the saucepan. Whisk until the pudding thickens. Remove from the heat and whisk in the butter and vanilla extract.

6. Pour the pudding into the crust and cover with plastic wrap. Refrigerate overnight.

TO MAKE THE QUANTUM WHIPPED CREAM:

7. Before serving, place all the whipped cream ingredients into a bowl and whip with a hand-mixer until it forms stiff peaks. Remove the plastic wrap from the pie and top with whipped cream.

DRINKS

NUKA-COLA

We are excited to bring you an entire line of Nuka-Cola products! Although we wanted to share the official secret recipe—including all 17 different fruits—we were unable to settle some legal differences between Vault-Tec™ and the Nuka-Cola Corporation. However, we've put our best scientists on the task and have come up with that cold refreshing Nuka-Cola taste with a 566 percent more efficient use of fruit! Consider it our gift to you!

S.P.E.C.I.A.L:
+1 ENDURANCE
FOR 30 MINUTES

DIFFICULTY:
EASY

PREP TIME:
12 HOURS

COOK TIME:
30 MINUTES

SERVINGS:
15 TO 20

PAIRS WELL WITH:
DUSTY'S BRAHMIN
BURGERS (PAGE 89)

2 cups water

3 cups sugar

Zest and juice of ½ orange

Zest and juice of ½ lime

Zest and juice of ½ lemon

1 cinnamon stick

3 cardamom pods

½ teaspoon coriander seed

2 star anise

¼ cup browning sauce

1 teaspoon vanilla extract

TO MAKE NUKA-COLA SYRUP:

1. Combine the water, sugar, orange zest, lime zest, lemon zest, cinnamon stick, cardamom pods, coriander seeds, and star anise in a large saucepan and place over medium-high heat. Whisk until the sugar has dissolved and then bring to a boil. Reduce the heat to low and simmer for 10 minutes.

2. Remove from the heat and strain into an airtight container. Add the orange, lime, and lemon juices (should be about ⅓ cup juice total). Mix in the browning sauce and vanilla extract. Once cooled, cover and store in refrigerator for at least 12 hours and up to 2 weeks.

TO MAKE AN ICE-COLD GLASS OF NUKA-COLA:

3. Combine 1 cup seltzer water, ice, and 5 to 7 tablespoons of Nuka-Cola syrup, then stir together.

NUKA-COLA QUANTUM

Our original Nuka-Cola Quantum recipe needed a few more exotic ingredients, but as these are required for vault power and coolant operations, we've decided to include neon blue food dye in all kitchens instead.

S.P.E.C.I.A.L:
+1 INTELLIGENCE
FOR 30 MINUTES

DIFFICULTY:
EASY

PREP TIME:
12 HOURS

COOK TIME:
30 MINUTES

SERVINGS:
15 TO 20

PAIRS WELL WITH:
MISSISSIPPI QUANTUM
PIE (PAGE 159)

1 cup water

2 cups sugar

Zest and juice of 1 lemon

Zest and juice of 1 lime

2 tablespoons fruit punch

2 tablespoons pomegranate juice

1 teaspoon citric acid

5 drops neon blue food dye

TO MAKE NUKA-COLA QUANTUM SYRUP:

1. Combine the water, sugar, lemon zest, lime zest, fruit punch, and pomegranate juice in a medium saucepan and place over medium-high heat. Whisk until the sugar has dissolved and then bring to a boil. Reduce the heat to low and simmer for 10 minutes.

2. Remove from the heat and strain into an airtight container. Add the lime and lemon juice. Mix in the citric acid and food dye. Once cooled, cover and store in refrigerator for at least 12 hours and up to 2 weeks.

TO MAKE AN ICE-COLD GLASS OF NUKA-COLA QUANTUM:

3. Combine 1 cup seltzer water, ice, and 9 tablespoons of Nuka-Cola Quantum syrup, then stir together.

Bottle and Cappy

NUKA-CHERRY

I SAW A SPECIAL-EDITION CHERRY FLAVORED BOTTLE OF NUKA-COLA IN DIAMOND CITY AND WANTED TO BRING SOME BACK. AFTER LOOKING EVERYWHERE, NONE OF THE VENDING MACHINES I STUMBLED ACROSS HAD ANY, SO I FIGURED I'D THROW TOGETHER A CHERRY VARIANT MYSELF!

S.P.E.C.I.A.L:
+1 LUCK
FOR 30 MINUTES

DIFFICULTY:
EASY

PREP TIME:
12 HOURS

COOK TIME:
30 MINUTES

SERVINGS:
10 TO 15

PAIRS WELL WITH:
MYSTERY MEAT–WRAPPED
NUKALURK (PAGE 31)

1½ cups water

1 cup sugar

1 cup pitted fresh cherries, halved

TO MAKE NUKA-CHERRY SYRUP:

1. Combine the water, sugar, and cherries in a medium saucepan and place over medium-high heat. Whisk until the sugar has dissolved and then bring to a boil. Reduce the heat to low and simmer for 20 minutes.

2. Remove from the heat and strain into an airtight container. Once cooled, cover and store in refrigerator for at least 12 hours and up to 2 weeks.

TO MAKE AN ICE-COLD GLASS OF NUKA-CHERRY:

3. Combine 1 cup seltzer water, 5 tablespoons Nuka-Cherry syrup, 4 tablespoons Nuka-Cola syrup (page 165), and ice, then stir together.

NUKA-COLA QUARTZ

Another refreshing twist on your favorite soft drink, this time
with a smooth vanilla taste.

S.P.E.C.I.A.L:
+1 AGILITY
FOR 30 MINUTES

DIFFICULTY:
EASY

PREP TIME:
12 HOURS

COOK TIME:
30 MINUTES

SERVINGS:
15 TO 20

PAIRS WELL WITH:
MOLE RAT WONDER
MEAT DIP (PAGE 23)

1 cup water

2 cups sugar

1 vanilla bean, split and scraped

1 tablespoon vanilla extract

TO MAKE NUKA-COLA QUARTZ SYRUP:

1. Combine the water, sugar, and vanilla bean in a
   medium saucepan and place over medium-high heat.
   Whisk until the sugar has dissolved and then bring
   to a boil. Remove from the heat and add the vanilla
   extract.

2. Once cooled, place in an airtight container. Cover
   and store in refrigerator for at least 12 hours and up
   to 2 weeks.

TO MAKE AN ICE-COLD GLASS OF NUKA-COLA QUARTZ:

3. Combine 1 cup seltzer water, 4 tablespoons Nuka-Cola Quartz syrup,
   1 tablespoon heavy cream, and ice. Stir to combine.

NUKA-COLA FLOAT

Miss going out to the local diner and ordering your favorite float? Don't just sit there, make your own! Craft your own ice cream and customize your Nuka-Cola float with the syrup that best describes you. Who are you? Feeling a bit cherry? Or perhaps vanilla is more your style?

S.P.E.C.I.A.L:
+1 PERCEPTION
FOR 30 MINUTES

DIFFICULTY:
EASY

PREP TIME:
1 DAY

COOK TIME:
20 MINUTES

SERVINGS:
4

PAIRS WELL WITH:
DEATHCLAW WELLINGHAM
(PAGE 101)

ICE CREAM:

2 cups heavy cream

1 cup half-and-half

¾ cup sugar

Pinch of salt

1 vanilla bean, split and scraped

1 cinnamon stick

2 star anise

FLOAT:

2 scoops of vanilla ice cream

Prepared Nuka-Cola soda of choice

TO MAKE THE ICE CREAM:

1. Combine the heavy cream, half-and-half, sugar, and salt in a medium saucepan. Place over medium-high heat and stir to combine. Add the vanilla bean, cinnamon stick, and star anise. Bring to a low boil, but make sure to stir frequently to keep the milk from sticking to the pan. Reduce the heat to low and simmer for 20 minutes, stirring frequently.

2. Transfer the mixture to a medium bowl and allow it to cool before covering, and refrigerate for at least 1 hour. Follow the instructions of your ice cream maker to make the ice cream, then place in a freezer-safe container and let it freeze overnight. Prior to serving, remove the ice cream from the freezer for 10 minutes for an easier scoop.

TO MAKE THE FLOAT:

3. Chill a tall glass in the freezer for 30 minutes. Add the ice cream scoops to the cold glass. Carefully pour the Nuka-Cola soda into the glass. Stir slightly and serve.

DEEZER'S **LEMONADE**

It's important that vault dwellers do not forsake basic nutrition. Get your fix of vitamin C with a cold, refreshing glass of lemonade!

S.P.E.C.I.A.L:
+1 CHARISMA
FOR 30 MINUTES

DIFFICULTY:
EASY

PREP TIME:
15 MINUTES

COOK TIME:
30 MINUTES

SERVINGS:
6

PAIRS WELL WITH:
IGUANA-ON-A-STICK
(PAGE 29)

3 to 4 cups water, divided

1 cup sugar

½ cup blueberries

½ cup blackberries

1½ cups fresh lemon juice

I REPLACED THESE BERRIES WITH A HANDFUL OF MUTFRUIT.

1. Make a simple syrup by combining 1 cup of the water and the sugar in a small saucepan over medium-high heat. Stir until the sugar has dissolved. Bring to a boil, reduce the heat to low, and simmer for 5 minutes. Remove from the heat and allow to cool.

2. Blend the blueberries and blackberries in a blender until liquified. Pour the fruit through a mesh strainer into a pitcher to remove any seeds. Add the syrup and lemon juice. Add 2 cups of water and taste. If it's too strong, add another cup of water.

I FOUND AN ODD ROBOT NAMED DEEZER WHO CLAIMED HIS LEMONADE WAS THE BEST IN THE ENTIRE UNITED STATES. HE THEN HANDED ME A MURKY PURPLE CONTAINER OF SOMETHING, UH, LIQUIDY? IT WASN'T THE WORST THING I'VE HAD BUT I DON'T THINK IT WAS LEMONADE.

VIM QUARTZ

Vault dweller, do we have a treat for you! Did you hear about Vim Quartz, the drink that never made it to store shelves because of a legal battle with the Nuka-Cola Corporation? We may have gotten our hands on a little sample of our own, and now we are giving the recipe to you. It's not like Vim! Pop Incorporated can do anything about it!

IT'S UNFORTUNATE THAT VIM! POP INCORPORATED LOST OUT IN COURT. THEIR DRINKS WERE FAR MORE UNIQUE THAN ANYTHING THE NUKA-COLA CORPORATION CREATED.

S.P.E.C.I.A.L:
+1 CHARISMA
FOR 1 HOUR

DIFFICULTY:
EASY

PREP TIME:
5 MINUTES

COOK TIME:
5 MINUTES

SERVINGS:
2

PAIRS WELL WITH:
BRAISED DEATHCLAW
STEAK (PAGE 97)

4 basil leaves

½ lime

Ice

¼ cup carrot juice

½ cup apple juice

½ cup ginger beer

ASH BLOSSOM SEEMS TO WORK WELL WITH THE FLAVORS FROM THE CARROTS AND APPLE IN THIS RECIPE.

1. Muddle the basil leaves in a cocktail shaker. Juice the lime into the shaker. Fill with ice and add the carrot juice and apple juice. Cover and shake for 10 seconds.

2. Fill two glasses with ice and divide the mixture between them. Add the ginger beer and stir slightly.

MELON SWAMPTAIL
FRESH MELON SQUEEZE

The perfect drink for the kids. Let them feel like an adult without the alcohol!

THE McCLELLAN FAMILY'S MISTER HANDY IS REALLY INTO MELONS. HE KEPT OFFERING DIFFERENT MELON-FLAVORED MEALS AND DRINKS SO I SHOWED HIM THIS RECIPE AND HE GOT EXTREMELY EXCITED. HE WON'T STOP MAKING THEM NOW.

S.P.E.C.I.A.L:
+1 ENDURANCE
FOR 1 HOUR

DIFFICULTY:
EASY

PREP TIME:
5 MINUTES

COOK TIME:
5 MINUTES

SERVINGS:
1

PAIRS WELL WITH:
SLOW-ROASTED
LEG OF YAO GUAI
(PAGE 111)

3 spoonfuls horned melon

¼ cup ginger beer

½ cup limeade

Splash of grenadine

MELON SEEMS TO HAVE MADE IT IN THE WASTELAND. IF LEFT TO RIPEN LONG ENOUGH, THE INSIDES SEEM TO TRANSFORM INTO THE GREEN GOOP LIKE THE PICTURE.

1. Add the horned melon to a glass. Pour the ginger beer and limeade over the melon. Stir slightly. Add a splash of grenadine and serve.

VIM REFRESH

Here is a tasty drink from Vim! Pop Incorporated. This refreshing appletini-inspired cocktail is perfect for that 5 o'clock feeling, no matter where you are. At the local tap house? Hunkered with your family in fear as the sound of nuclear death rains down around you? Lounging in our state-of-the-art vaults? You'll always find a good excuse to enjoy this recipe.

S.P.E.C.I.A.L:
+1 STRENGTH
FOR 30 MINUTES

DIFFICULTY:
EASY

PREP TIME:
1 TO 3 DAYS

COOK TIME:
10 MINUTES

SERVINGS:
2

PAIRS WELL WITH:
MULLED PEARS
(PAGE 119)

One 1-inch piece fresh ginger,
    peeled and thinly sliced
½ cup vodka
½ cup apple schnapps
Splash of sweet vermouth
Ice
Apple slices for garnishing

1. Place the ginger and vodka in a sealable container. Seal and shake gently. Set aside and allow to infuse for 1 to 3 days in a cool, dark place.

2. Remove the ginger and combine the infused vodka, apple schnapps, vermouth, and ice in a cocktail shaker. Cover and shake for 10 seconds. Strain into a chilled glass. Garnish with apple slices.

BERRY AND WHISKEY

When you're secluded underground, scurvy is no joke. Why not throw in a
punchline with some whiskey to wash it all down?

*I HAD SOMETHING SIMILAR AT SALVATORE'S BAR OVER IN NEW RENO, BUT THEY
CALLED IT A DIRTY WASTELANDER. HONESTLY, I COULDN'T TELL IF IT WAS AN
INSULT OR A TERM OF ENDEARMENT, BUT IT WAS QUITE TASTY NONETHELESS.*

S.P.E.C.I.A.L:
+3 STRENGTH,
-2 INTELLIGENCE
FOR 30 MINUTES

DIFFICULTY:
EASY

PREP TIME:
5 MINUTES

COOK TIME:
5 MINUTES

SERVINGS:
3

PAIRS WELL WITH:
MIRELURK BELLY
CROQUETTES (PAGE 21)

4 blackberries

4 blueberries

2 tablespoons Nuka-Cola syrup
(page 165)

3 tablespoons Nuka-Cherry syrup
(page 168)

3 tablespoons whiskey

Ice

½ cup club soda

1. Place the blueberries and blackberries in a cocktail
   shaker. Mash the berries to release the juices. Add
   the Nuka-Cola syrup, Nuka-Cherry syrup, whiskey,
   and ice. Shake vigorously for 10 seconds. Using
   a fine-mesh strainer, strain into 3 serving glasses
   filled with ice. Top with the club soda.

VIM CAPTAIN'S BLEND

We have another Vault-Tec™ exclusive drink recipe for you, the legendary Vim Captain's Blend! It's never been fully released to the public, but we've secured a recipe to re-create that fishy, I-just-fell-off-a-pier taste you've heard so much about.

FISH, TOMATO JUICE, AND ALCOHOL? IS THIS A DRINK OR A SOUP?

S.P.E.C.I.A.L:
+1 AGILITY
FOR 30 MINUTES

DIFFICULTY:
MEDIUM

PREP TIME:
10 MINUTES

COOK TIME:
5 MINUTES

SERVINGS:
1

PAIRS WELL WITH:
BRUNCH

¼ cup plus 2 tablespoons vodka

⅔ cup clamato juice

2 dashes Worcestershire sauce

1 dash tabasco sauce

Juice of ¼ lime

Juice of ¼ lemon

⅛ teaspoon celery salt

⅛ teaspoon garlic powder

1 teaspoon fish sauce

1 bacon strip, cooked, for garnishing

1 crab claw, cooked, for garnishing

1 celery rib, for garnishing

1. In a large measuring cup, combine the vodka, clamato juice, Worcestershire sauce, tabasco, lime juice, lemon juice, celery salt, garlic powder, and fish sauce, and stir together.

2. Fill a serving glass with ice and place the garnishes inside, then pour in the drink.

SURFACE – NEVER!

VAULT – FOREVER!

Ware's Brew MAPLE JULEP

In honor of the greatest race in the world, the Kentucky Derby,
Vault-Tec™ invites you to make this drink to celebrate derby lovers everywhere.

WE HAVE SOME DERBY-WINNING TOY CARS LAYING AROUND THE VAULT. I'M NOT
SURE HOW A BUNCH OF WOODEN CARS COULD HAVE BEEN SUCH A SPECTACLE TO BE
CALLED THE "GREATEST RACE IN THE WORLD," BUT TO EACH THEIR OWN I SUPPOSE.

S.P.E.C.I.A.L:
+1 CHARISMA
FOR 30 MINUTES

DIFFICULTY:
EASY

PREP TIME:
5 MINUTES

COOK TIME:
5 MINUTES

SERVINGS:
1

PAIRS WELL WITH:
A DERBY PARTY

5 mint leaves, plus more for garnishing

2 tablespoons maple syrup

¼ cup bourbon

½ cup club soda

Crushed ice

1. Muddle the mint and maple syrup in an old-fashioned glass. Add the bourbon and club soda. Fill with crushed ice and stir. Garnish with additional mint leaves.

ELDERFLOWER SIPPER ~ Rot Gut

Relive those grand memories of relaxing on the veranda with a cool drink in hand! Please remember that consuming alcohol outside the vault premises is forbidden as it requires leaving the vault.

THE FOLKS OUT WEST STARTED OUTFITTING THEIR VEHICLES WITH ROT GUT ENGINES TO GET AROUND. A WASTE OF A TASTY DRINK IF YOU ASK ME.

S.P.E.C.I.A.L:
-2 PERCEPTION,
THEN +2 PERCEPTION

DIFFICULTY:
EASY

PREP TIME:
5 MINUTES

COOK TIME:
5 MINUTES

SERVINGS:
1

PAIRS WELL WITH:
SEAFOOD

¼ cup vodka

1 tablespoon elderflower liqueur

¼ cup cranberry juice

Ice

Club soda

1. Combine the vodka, elderflower liqueur, and cranberry juice in a cocktail shaker filled with ice. Cover and shake vigorously for 10 seconds. Strain into a highball glass with fresh ice. Top with club soda.

HOT TODDY

One sip of this will help soothe any cough.

THIS RECIPE REMINDS ME OF A DRINK I HAD AT THE LAST PLANK UP NORTH OFF THE COAST OF MAINE. THEY CALLED IT FIRE BELLY, AND BOY DOES IT LIVE UP TO THAT NAME. IT MADE ME READY FOR A FIGHT!

S.P.E.C.I.A.L:
+1 ENDURANCE
FOR 1 HOUR

DIFFICULTY:
EASY

PREP TIME:
30 MINUTES

COOK TIME:
30 MINUTES

SERVINGS:
1

PAIRS WELL WITH:
A COLD

SPICED SYRUP:

½ cup water

1 cup sugar

1 cinnamon stick

1 strip orange peel

1 strip lime peel

2 slices fresh peeled ginger

1 whole clove

HOT TODDY:

1 black tea bag

1 cup boiling water

1 tablespoon honey

2 tablespoons spiced syrup

3 tablespoons whiskey

1 tablespoon lemon juice

TO MAKE THE SPICED SYRUP:

1. Combine all of the spiced syrup ingredients in a saucepan and place over medium-high heat. Whisk until the sugar has dissolved and then bring to a boil. Reduce the heat to low and simmer for 20 minutes. Remove from the heat and strain into an airtight container. Once cooled, cover and store in the refrigerator for up to 2 weeks.

TO MAKE THE HOT TODDY:

2. In a mug, brew the black tea with the hot water. Stir in the honey, spiced syrup, whiskey, and lemon juice. Stir until the honey dissolves.

TEQUILA SUNRISE

Daddy-O

I came across some . . . creative types living in Goodneighbor who were really into this chem called Daddy-O. I didn't touch the stuff but suggested they try exploring some different horizons with something a bit less hazardous to their health by trying this tasty cocktail.

S.P.E.C.I.A.L:
+3 INTELLIGENCE,
+3 PERCEPTION
FOR 30 MINUTES

DIFFICULTY:
EASY

PREP TIME:
5 MINUTES

COOK TIME:
5 MINUTES

SERVINGS:
1

PAIRS WELL WITH:
MIRELURK CLAW CAKES
(PAGE 35), SPICED
MIRELURK MEAT (PAGE 95)

Ice

¼ cup tequila

¼ cup grapefruit juice

¼ cup orange juice

1 tablespoon grenadine

1. Fill a highball glass with ice. Stir in the tequila, grapefruit juice, and orange juice. Slowly pour in the grenadine and let it settle to the bottom.

STIMPAK

Feeling a little under the weather? Nothing like a good stimpak to get you up and going!

S.P.E.C.I.A.L:
+3 ENDURANCE
FOR 30 MINUTES

DIFFICULTY:
MEDIUM

PREP TIME:
6 HOURS

COOK TIME:
30 MINUTES

SERVINGS:
THIRTEEN 2.5-ML
SYRINGES

PAIRS WELL WITH:
HUMAN MISHAPS

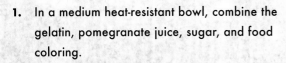

BRAHMIN HOOVES ARE
A GOOD REPLACEMENT
HERE.

2 tablespoons unflavored gelatin

¼ cup pomegranate juice

¼ cup sugar

3 drops red food coloring

1 cup water

¾ cup cold raspberry vodka

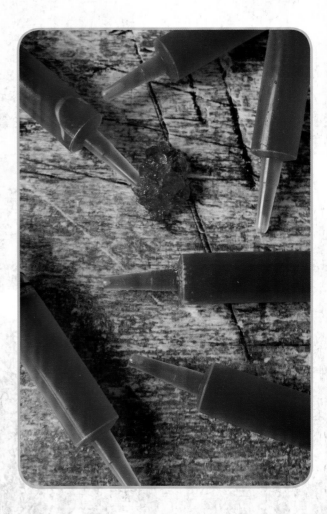

1. In a medium heat-resistant bowl, combine the gelatin, pomegranate juice, sugar, and food coloring.

2. Bring the water to a boil in a small pan then pour the water into the bowl with the gelatin and stir until the gelatin has fully dissolved.

3. Add the raspberry vodka and mix well. Pour the mixture into 2.5-ounce syringes. Refrigerate for at least 5 hours before serving.

NUKA-BOMBDROP

~~LONG ISLAND~~

I CAME ACROSS AN OLD ROBOT AT AN ABANDONED TAP HOUSE IN BOSTON THAT WAS DESIGNED TO CRAFT DRINKS. I WANTED TO TAKE THE DRINKIN' BUDDY BACK TO THE VAULT WITH ME BUT I COULDN'T SNEAK HIM BY ALL THE BANDITS IN THE AREA. I DID MANAGE TO GET A FEW PRETTY UNIQUE DRINK RECIPES FROM IT BEFORE I HAD TO ESCAPE.

S.P.E.C.I.A.L:
+1 PERCEPTION
FOR 1 HOUR

DIFFICULTY:
EASY

PREP TIME:
10 MINUTES

COOK TIME:
5 MINUTES

SERVINGS:
2

PAIRS WELL WITH:
DUSTY'S BRAHMIN
BURGERS (PAGE 89),
HOT DOGS

½ lemon

½ lime

Ice

½ tablespoon triple sec

2 tablespoons gin

2 tablespoons rum

2 tablespoons vodka

2 tablespoons tequila

2 dashes bitters

Prepared Nuka-Cola soda (page 165)

1. Juice the lemon and lime into a cocktail shaker. Fill with ice and add the triple sec, gin, rum, vodka, tequila, and bitters. Cover and shake for 10 seconds. Pour, including the ice, into two highball glasses. Fill each cup with Nuka-Cola soda. Garnish with lemon and lime slices.

RADAWAY

If you are ever feeling a bit down, make yourself a RadAway
and watch that uranium fever vanish.

1 lime, quartered

Dash of ground allspice

Ice

¼ cup dark rum

¼ cup Nuka-Cola soda (page 165)

Club soda

1. Squeeze the juice of three lime wedges into a
   highball glass. Add the allspice and stir. Add
   the ice and pour the rum over the ice. Place
   one of the lime wedges in the cup and fill with
   Prepared Nuka-Cola soda. Stir lightly.

S.P.E.C.I.A.L.

The perfect punch to bring to any adult party.
We guarantee you'll feel S.P.E.C.I.A.L. after partaking.

SURE, THIS DRINK INCREASES YOUR STATS, BUT THE AFTER EFFECTS CAN REALLY SLOW YOU DOWN DURING COMBAT.

S.P.E.C.I.A.L:
+1 TO EACH STAT
FOR 4 HOURS

DIFFICULTY:
EASY

PREP TIME:
30 MINUTES

COOK TIME:
10 MINUTES

SERVINGS:
MANY

PAIRS WELL WITH:
S.P.E.C.I.A.L. PARTY

½ cup water

1 cup Sugar

1½ cups Pomegranate juice

½ cup Elderflower liqueur

7 cups Champagne or sparkling wine

3 cups Ice

1 cup Apple cider

2 Lemons, sliced

1. Combine the water and sugar in a small saucepan over medium-high heat. Stir until the sugar has dissolved. Bring to a boil, reduce the heat to low, and simmer for 5 minutes. Take off the heat and allow the syrup to cool.

2. Combine the pomegranate juice, elderflower liqueur, champagne, and apple cider in a pitcher or punch bowl. Add the syrup slowly, tasting as you go to reach the desired sweetness. Add the lemon slices and ice. Serve immediately.

INSIGHT
EDITIONS

PO Box 3088
San Rafael, CA 94912
www.insighteditions.com

f Find us on Facebook: www.facebook.com/InsightEditions
x Follow us on Twitter: @insighteditions

Library of Congress Cataloging-in-Publication Data available.

ISBN: 978-1-68383-397-0

Publisher: Raoul Goff
Associate Publisher: Vanessa Lopez
Creative Director: Chrissy Kwasnik
Designer: Evelyn Furuta
Senior Editor: Amanda Ng
Editorial Assistant: Maya Alpert
Senior Production Editor: Rachel Anderson
Production Manager: Greg Steffen

ROOTS of PEACE   REPLANTED PAPER

Insight Editions, in association with Roots of Peace, will plant two trees for
each tree used in the manufacturing of this book. Roots of Peace is an
internationally renowned humanitarian organization dedicated to eradicating
land mines worldwide and converting war-torn lands into productive farms
and wildlife habitats. Roots of Peace will plant two million fruit and nut trees in
Afghanistan and provide farmers there with the skills and support necessary
for sustainable land use.

Manufactured in China by Insight Editions

10 9 8 7 6 5 4 3

ABOUT THE AUTHOR

Victoria Rosenthal launched her blog, Pixelated Provisions,
in 2012 to combine her lifelong passions for video games
and food by re-creating consumables found in many of
her favorite games. When she isn't experimenting in the
kitchen and dreaming up new recipes, she spends her days
developing graphics for NASA. She resides in Houston,
Texas, with her husband and corgi.

ACKNOWLEDGMENTS

Thanks to my Four Leaf Clovers: Jeff Rosenthal, Richard
Poskozim, Chris Lytle, Mike Rosenthal, Harry Readinger,
and Kanji. Thanks to my Lead Belly friends for being both
hungry and supportive: Irvin Chavira, Rene Rodriguez,
Kevin Gittens, Kevin McClure, Nick Esparza, Keenan
Maistry, Flor and Travis Kelly, Kevin Stich, Matt Thomas,
Brandon Quiocho, Forrest Porter, Joseph Vacca, and
William Baker.